NADENE JOY
INTERNATIONAL, BEST-SELLING
AUTHOR, CEC GLOBAL AMBASSADOR,
FOUNDER OF THE GLOBAL MOVEMENT
OF HOPE

AND

OTHER AUTHORS WHO SHARED THEIR
STORIES

The Power of Hope:
A Lifeline in Times of Uncertainty

Legal Disclaimer

Connect with MPowered Voice Publishing
www.MPoweredvoicepublishing.ca

DEDICATION

This book is dedicated to all the people in the world who are feeling hopeless and stuck as if there is no way out of their current situation. May you know that hope coupled with willful action, faith, and God's infinite unconditional love is light, and the truth you seek is within and is much closer than you think.

THE POWER OF HOPE

Acknowledgements

First and foremost, I would like to thank God, my eternal Heavenly Father in heaven, as with Him alone, All things are possible.

The world is a better place thanks to the many people who bring hope to others in ways big and small and in ways most don't even realize, such as a gentle smile, word of encouragement or pat on the back. It is through taking deliberate and mindful action through every word, behaviour, gesture and reaction to each situation that matters most and leads us either towards or away from greater unity will all. Thank-you to everyone who has gone through the numerous peaks and sometimes endless valleys and those who have boldly and courageously shared their story and message of Hope with the world. The many lessons we each have shared will live on to continue to help others move from the dark to the light at the end of the tunnel so that they know they are not alone, potentially for several generations to come hereafter.

To all the people I have had the privilege and honour of working with, leading and being mentored by over the years, I want to thank you for inspiring the writing of this book of Hope.

I would like to especially thank my dear family, my precious children, and many friends and my soul family from across the world, for I love each and every one of you dearly. Your immense guidance, unconditional love and support, faith and the hope you have provided along this journey called life is appreciated more than words can say.

Lastly, I would like to take a moment to thank my incredibly talented editor, extraordinary publisher and a special tribute of gratitude to the Legendary Les Brown, #1 motivational speaker in the world, for the writing the foreword for this book of Hope as you have been such an instrumental part in my life and journey.

THE POWER OF HOPE

TABLE OF CONTENTS

Contents

Dedication iii

Acknowledgements v

Table of Contents... vii

Foreword xi

Introduction xiii

The Art of Learning Life 1

Aliza Ansari *4*

Hope... 5

Carmel Bell.. *6*

The Life of JunNk.. 7

Sam McGowan.. *15*

Stop Settling – Answer Your Calling and Overcome Obstacles! 17

Meera Shah *25*

My Story of Hope 27

Brian Schulman *32*

What We Are Here Learning Is What We Are Here To Teach 35

Sally Anderson.. *48*

A Journey of Profound Lessons Through Time 49

By Brian J. Esposito 49

Brian Esposito *52*

A Choice to Surrender 55

Emily Rodger *64*

Hope is A Blind Trust in Action.. 65

By Amb. Chukwuemeka Innocent Amadi.. 65

Amb. Chukwuemeka Innocent Amadi.. 70

Every person we killed, it was because I said it was okay 71

Erika Andresen.. 78

Why Does Hope Matter? 79

By Manjit Kaur.. 79

Manjit Kaur 84

Born To Grow or Growing Into the Miracle You Are............................ 85

By Jason W. Freeman.. 85

Jason W. Freeman.. 89

When I Was Given 5 Years to Live... 91

Leanne Kabat.. 101

Hope As the Tree of Life... 103

By MD Samir Hasan... 103

MD Samir Hasan... 106

Finding your THRIVE.. 107

Nancy Barrows M.S CCC SLP... 118

If I Can, You Can 121

Aly Francis 131

Shining lights of hope in the shadows of religious extremism 133

Junaid Qaiser 138

Recovery is a Marathon 141

Jody Salway.. 144

MY HOPE 145

Faye Marks 146

The Four Pillars of Unity.. 147

Overcoming Covid Through Hope and Faith: A Story of The Gift of Life in Uncertain Times 151

Conclusion 155

Nadene Joy *157*

Hope Quotes 159

THE POWER OF HOPE

FOREWORD

How healthy are you? We know good health is more important than money, status, or possessions, yet, we continue to pursue things outside of our purpose and omit our health in the process.

There is something in the air. Do you smell it? Maybe you can feel it? And if you are not careful, you can be infected by it. Infected by the wave of negativity, stinking thinking, self-doubt, and fear. Somehow or another, the virus can be highly contagious and lingers if you do not protect yourself from it. Now more than ever, it is imperative to change your mind set in order to change your life, protect yourself, and combat the virus. Negativity must die along with the parasite's low self-worth, and toxic relationships.

No matter what, I am a firm believer of possibility thinking. It's Possible and It's Not Over Until You Win are among my most famous and impactful quotes, but change cannot occur unless there is Hope.

This book, its content, and the brilliance of its authors poured their most professional and personal transparency within these pages. This masterpiece will inspire anyone to a healthier lifestyle, provide an enhanced physical awareness, and advice for overall wellness.

More than 20 years ago, I heard the most feared words around the world, Les, you have cancer. What a slap in the face I thought. Why me? I questioned. My life hit a low point. I was at the height of my career, I still had young children, and I felt robbed. Looking back, the cancer diagnosis was my hope for turning things around. As a 20-year cancer conqueror, my journey to getting well began with the fear of dying too soon. I listened to my doctors and I listened more to positive messages and quotes. The thought of having cancer alone almost killed me. I made it a point to search for hope, survivors, and answers to beat cancer. I had to kill the bacteria of doubt in my mind.

For me, this book has cracked the secret code for mental and physical success. It does not include waving a magic wand, clicking your heels three times, or throwing a penny into a wishing well. It is a formula requiring more than the typical concentrate on your health, goals, and thinking happy thoughts; the authors present life changing information and challenges us to focus on our mission with an incredible effort and sustained action over time, in order to get maximized potential, which is changing the world!

There is a cure for this viral infection and if the pages within this book are applied correctly, your wit, grit, and stamina will improve. You will find your confidence at an all-time high and you will yield positive results. The method is equivalent to a modern-day Einstein strategy. Each contributor has their own proven track record for their own personal and professional achievements and are capable of adding value to your life.

From personal experience, perseverance, nerve and discipline include some of the many requirements to help you reach your mountaintop and high places in life. As we know, ultimate success takes time.; maximized potential takes even longer, and oftentimes most people simply graze the surface of their true talents, and they are miserable.

Again, I must ask, How healthy are you? If you cannot honestly answer that question, I urge you to immediately turn to the next page quickly, let's get you healthy, empowered, and ready to become an agent of change for yourself, community, and the world at large.

I once heard, Consult not your fears but your hopes and your dreams. Think not about your frustrations, but about your unfulfilled potential. Concern yourself not with what you tried and failed in, but with what it is still possible for you to do.

You are going to have to fight to reach your destination. We are collectively at the Turning Point, do not get left behind. Always remember, It's possible, There is Hope! It may get hard, but do it hard. See you at the top.

Yours in greatness,
Les Brown
www.LesBrown.com

INTRODUCTION

Nadene Joy

In times of darkness, chaos and uncertainty, hope can be a lifeline, offering a source of strength and inspiration. It can help us stay focused on our goals, even when the path ahead is uncertain or difficult.

Ultimately, hope is a reminder that we are not alone and that we have the power to make a positive difference in the world. By holding onto hope and working towards a better today and future, we can create a more just, inclusive, and compassionate world for all.

As we begin this book of Hope, you are solemnly invited to begin in silent reflection on what Hope personally means to you. You can think more deeply about what makes you feel hopeful, what brings you hope, how you can help others experience greater hope, and what the advantages of Hope are, just to name a few topics to begin to ponder. Oftentimes when we think of hope, we go about our days and live living automatically without the innate realization that we have been subconsciously programmed by society, the world, the media, and even our close friends and family to believe the illusion that hope exists outside of ourselves and occurs sometime in the later future of our lives outside of the present moment. Taking this one step further, we have all likely heard at one or several times in our lives the saying, "Hope for tomorrow." The majority of our population globally, after hearing this over and over and over again, have taken this statement of Hope unknowingly as the ultimate truth, which may or may not prove to be true for each individual in society. Hope for "tomorrow" is something that creates future-based expectations of outcomes that many times are only illusionary facades that do not manifest into our everyday reality. The fact is that a part of the purpose of the writing of this book is to begin to challenge our individual deep-seated beliefs and ideologies and, in this case, our belief around what "true hope" really is and to move towards a more empowering existing present reality which is defined and relaxed on all levels in each moment with "hope for TODAY." We often think that Hope is outcome-based and can only exist in the future state. For example, when we do something tomorrow or next week or even next year, then we will have hope. If we do x, then we will have x. For example, when we are finally able to land that perfect ideal job, when we are no longer suffering from a debilitating illness, when we have the ideal partner or relationship of our dreams, when we make x number of dollars, when we get to travel the world, etc, the list is infinitely exhaustively endless. We begin to jump on a cycle that never ends and are always living for tomorrow with constant worry, doubt, anxiety and the fear of the unknown uncertainties of the future. This occurs in our life until we suddenly rejoice as we realize this no longer has to become the never-ending cycle we get stuck in. We all have been at a point in our lives where we are no longer living and enjoying our lives to the fullest in the "present moment," doing what we can and taking ACTION towards our greatest dreams and desires. That ultimately will be the first stepping stone to move us authentically and consistently towards our purpose in life. In doing this and choosing to start with the first step, we are able to bring greater hope for TODAY through a new concept I have coined, "ACTIONABLE HOPE." For example, if we want to be healthier, we can start by drinking half a glass of water more each day or doing one more push-up or arm curl than yesterday. Be more focused on becoming a better version of yourself than you were yesterday and focus less on competing with others and more on greater alignment with your own personal morals and values, as this brings not just temporary but long-term Hope into our lives. We can look back each day with complete compassion for ourselves and others with no judgement on the one or more things we improved upon and took ACTION towards compared with the day before. Know that no one is perfect, and if you miss a day, it is okay — just make sure to get back on track as soon as you can to keep the momentum of hope and action moving forward. When we choose to act and speak with greater love and compassion to all others, we will awaken another's soul to where Hope exists. When we choose to live with intentionality and know that our actions matter, and live our life to its fullest in each circumstance in every present moment, we experience many things, including, first and foremost, greater faith and belief in self, which leads to increased hope on all levels. This inadvertently also increases our sense of peace, love, faith, joy and an overall purpose in our lives. You are greater than you think.

No matter where in the world you live or what your status, Hope prevails in the darkest of times and sheds light and truth to an otherwise hopeless situation. However, the reality is that when we become consciously aware of what is going on deep below the surface in ourselves, we have learned to operate and behave in certain ways that may no longer be healthy or beneficial for ourselves and others. We now have the empowered option to make a conscious choice in each moment to choose to move towards having hope today and in each moment of every day moving forward.

What is Hope, and Why Does it Matter?

Hope is a relatively simple word; however, having it can make a world of difference. When everything in life fails, it can be the solid anchor that helps you hold on and push through rather than letting go and giving up. *"It is the force that binds your dreams and aspirations to your willpower and strength."*

Hope vs Faith

We like to think and experience "hope" as an optimistic attitude towards something we expect. "Faith," on the other hand, is a "feeling of confidence or trust in something that we believe in." Nonetheless, the two of these go hand-in-hand in life, regardless of the challenges you are currently facing or have gone through in the past. Hope and Faith, coupled together with action, are unstoppable.

There Are No Coincidences in Life

Most people don't know that my first name Nadene, means Hope. Growing up as a small child in Canada, I knew at a very young age that I was different and had an inner fire to want to help empower people to live more joyful healthy lives in many ways, but I could just not put my finger on what exactly this was and how it would happen. As I grew older into adulthood and learned more about my identity and who I was, I slowly began to understand more. I began to recognize that not all the beliefs I held were my own, and I started to question why I believed what I did, acted the way I did and even thought the thoughts I thought in each moment. It became apparently clear that I had taken on the perceptions of others, including those of society, media, friends, family, teachers, and many others I had come in contact with over my lifetime up until this point, as my ultimate truth. I had to begin to let go of many things that no longer served me for my highest good and all those around me, one of which was the need and illusionary unrealistic desire for perfection. I realized I had an unresolved belief of not feeling good enough that I was carrying was not my own. My strong desire for perfection was rooted in this belief that wasn't even my own and existed from being passed down from my generational lineage. It gave me hope. I'm now knowing the truth as the first step to creating lasting change always begins with awareness first. I now had the acute awareness and recognition and blessing of knowing from my firsthand experiences that not everything is as it seems. As I grew up and went through my journey of becoming, I experienced many peaks and numerous valleys of struggle in my life. Many character-building and powerful life lessons were learned that have moulded and shaped me into the person and humble leader I am today.

The times we are living in are filled with much uncertainty, which is why remaining informed, optimistic, and flexible is more important now than ever before. *"Optimism is the faith that leads to achievement,"* said Helen Keller, a woman very familiar with insurmountable odds — as well as uncertain, scary times. *"Nothing,"* she continued, *"can be done without hope."*

Once we take the time to examine the reality of our own unique perspectives, we start to see the sheer power of hope alone, a subject often relegated to motivational speakers, wishful thinkers, yearbook quotes and greeting cards. However, a June 2020 Psychology Today article by Dr. David B. Feldman argues that hope isn't the same thing as wishful thinking. "It's not even the same as glass-half-full thinking," he says. "Hope is applicable even when the glass is only a third full or has nothing in it at all. That's because real hope isn't about living in a fantasy world; it's about living in this one. It doesn't deny suffering and pain." He asserts it's because hope isn't a delusion but rather something people very much grounded in the real world, who understand and accept that life can be tough, unfair, and chaotic, use to stay on course and create better realities for themselves. Hope isn't abstract. It's very concrete.

Hope helps us set GOALS.

Hope is "a way of thinking that pushes us to action." Research finds that when people have hope, they're more likely to make their goals a reality. When people have a clear belief, a clear hope, about what's possible, they're more likely to take the action needed on that goal to bring it to fruition.

People with hope are able to envision and pursue a future different than their current reality. They're able to set clear goals, develop multiple strategies to attain those goals, and stay motivated to reach those goals even when they experience setbacks.

Hope doesn't mean blind optimism. The Merriam Webster Dictionary defines hope simply as "to expect with confidence."

The difference between feeling hopeless vs hopeful

Hopelessness is a feeling of isolation that things will not and cannot change and creates a sense that there is no solution to a problem. Having Hope, on the other hand, is a belief in something greater, the possibility of something greater that unites us together in our lives and can be the one thing that changes and even possibly, one day, saves our life.

Hope is an incredible internal strength and protective factor in our lives.

How to bring greater hope into your life:

* Attend local and/or online support groups

* Counselling – talk to someone neutral or that you trust

* Use helplines for support

* Be mindful of what you eat, as this can help elevate your mood

* Exercise – this doesn't have to be at the gym – try walking, doing housework faster, or going up and down the stairs. Be realistic about your goals and abilities

* Practice mindfulness, meditation and prayer – you can download apps such as Headspace, Calm and the Bible app

* Practice getting into and setting a daily morning routine again

* Get into the habit of staying connected with others

* Helping others and focus on one good cause in your community- humanitarian work has been proven to benefit both parties- a win-win for all

* Engage in personal development and work towards learning new skills, as this keeps the mind active and engaged

* Do breathing exercises – relaxation breathing to calm the body, mind and soul

* Read more often and try going to the library

* Focus on the present moment and let go of all beliefs and things, including people who no longer bring positive, healthy behaviours into your world

Positive Impacts and The Many Advantages of Hope

* Hope has been proven to reduce feelings of helplessness, increase happiness, reduce stress, and overall improve our quality of life.

* Gives you a reason to get out of bed every day- start every day with the first goal of making your bed

* Improves mental and cognitive wellbeing

* Benefits your overall physical body and improves your physical health

* Increases your greater social network and supports

* Life quality is significantly improved, including life expectancy

* Increases immune system strength as it consistently reduces levels of stress

* Self-worth, self-belief and confidence all increase

* Encouragement for you to take positive action

* Reminds you to surround yourself with like-minded people

* Greatly reduces stress, depression, sadness and anxiety

* Creates vast opportunities

* Increases productivity and employee retention at work

* You are more able to handle greater pain and adversity then less hopeful peers

* Substantially Increases problem-solving ability

* Students with hope for their future, who can confidently expect their goals to become a reality, are less likely to drop out of school.

Sometimes we need help to see things in a different way, sometimes, we need to change parts of our lives, whatever it may be. There is support out there to help you find the strength to believe that hope is a possibility, and it can help us change the way that we live.

"Hope is calm, love, peace, health, forgiveness and acceptance for self and all others."

Hope and Predictors of Student Success

Dr. Valerie Maholmes states that there's no more important predictor of success than hope, especially in children who come from environments where all circumstantial evidence points to the contrary. She said that children who are able to adapt and overcome adversity tend to have a higher sense of self-efficacy, which feeds their sense of competency and leads to a feeling of control over their environment and destination. *"Hope is one big trickle-down effect."*

In discussing the results of Gallup's 2018 Survey of K-12 School District Superintendents, Gallup Senior Editor Dr. Jeffrey Jones found that according to the survey results, "students who are engaged — those involved and enthusiastic about school l— are more likely to be hopeful for the future and have better academic performance than their disengaged peers. Earlier Gallup surveys indicate that students stay engaged (which in turn keeps them in school) when they're able to connect what they're learning to their futures and thinking about their futures is what gives students that assumption that a positive outcome can happen — it's all interconnected.

"The takeaway then, for educators, mentors, family members, and anyone else helping prepare the next generation of workers for career and life success is to work your best to instill a sense of hope in that next generation, especially in these very uncertain times. It's not something that comes naturally to everyone but is something that can be cultivated and worked on."

In addition, hope is also just as important in the recovery from mental illness as in physical illness as hope becomes the foundational root and matters in all situations - the only difference is that in mental illness, the end point is much harder to rationalize in the mind because it requires an awareness that one's mental state is not fixed and can be changed with a conscious choice to do so. The truth being that mental illnesses are not part of one's nature, but rather, are states of mind which can be modified for the better and changed in many instances. As a concrete society as a whole and within each individual unit, we must ensure hope, and the belief in hope, is instilled in those suffering from mental illness because "hope offers the means by which a better future can be perceived; and therefore, achieved."

Next Steps Forward - Hope

You are enthusiastically personally invited to begin to look beyond the negative headlines of the news and media and our world as a whole to uncover the top reasons to have hope starting today for a brighter future.

Lessons of Hope

In times of difficulty and struggle, we often hear a lot about hope. Perhaps and to be honest, more than we'd like to admit, we are in the mood for. Have you ever personally felt like the worse things get, the more we're told to have hope? Hold on to hope, embrace it, and reach for it. Did you know that hope and exercise have many powerful qualities in common? Exercise has short - and long-term benefits and, most times, requires more persistence and discipline than we'd like. The trouble with this is that when it's being sold to us as being an easy fix without understanding why it's so important or what it takes to maintain in the longer term. It is the small action steps we take each day that, compounded over time, make the largest difference both inside and out. Whether it is exercise, hope, our eating habits, our mental mindset or daily spiritual mindful practices, the results always come after the small incremental steps we take each day. It is the choice we all have in this exact moment to choose to act and take diligent action towards our goals, our dreams, and live a life overflowing with meaningful purpose and greater unconditional love, peace, joy and unity for all. It all starts with you, having hope today.

Redefining HOPE - Helping Other People Elevate

Sometimes and more oftentimes than not, it is difficult to see the outward progress of our actions. When we are going through difficult times and keep getting beaten down, we can easily lose hope and many times, the finish line seems farther away than when we began. Hope seems nonexistent —sometimes, our hope feels small. This is where consciously choosing to take action, one small action, can move you in a positive direction back towards hope in the moment. It can be as simple as calling a friend to talk when you are having a bad day, choosing to drink one more glass of water today than you did yesterday, smiling at a stranger or holding the door at the grocery store.

When we take action and do something meaningful, no matter how small, in service from the heart, we bring hope, elevate and inspire and become positive role models to others to also do the same or greater. In return, we almost magically also bring greater Hope into our own lives throughout the process. This is one of the ingredients in the recipe of fostering greater hope which always comes back to keeping things simple and helping other people elevate, either physically, emotionally, spiritually or within all three areas of their life combined. When we help others, we help ourselves.

In order for each of us to begin to move and work towards a world of greater justice, kindness, respect and love for all people, we first have to believe it's possible, even if the road ahead will be long. We must have a solid faith and believe with God all things are possible. If we have even just the tiniest ounce of hope, we can start to move forward on the journey and purpose we are destined to live out. If we are rooted in hope through God's almighty grace, we can keep going. We are the change we want to see in the world.

Do not Fear- Hope as the Anchor

Hope is the anchor that gives us the strength to keep going through injustice and heartbreak. It's a persistent, even stubborn, belief that there are still good things to come.

Fear bellows to us that the world is lost, chaotic and is ending before our existence. Hope counters this and summons thoughts that the story isn't over yet.

When we become afraid, we struggle to protect ourselves. We want certainty, guarantees and assurances instead of the quiet calm, sense of peace and eternal serenity that hope offers. We need to know that we cannot escape this imprisonment through our strength alone. We need something much stronger and more powerful.

"When our HOPE is rooted in FAITH, it's stronger than fear."

What this means is not that we will always be free of fear, however, it does mean that fear loses its control and power over us because our hope in God is the best defence against whatever comes against us. Even and especially when our hope in the midst of our greatest tribulations and struggles in life feels small, it's great enough to keep fear, doubt, worry and confusion of the event of darkness from overpowering us.

HOPE IS...

Hope is the light that shines bright, as where there is faith, the dark simply cannot exist.

Hope can always be found. It is present in every situation.

Hope is crying out to be heard, seen, and experienced.

Hope is never lost.

For in this hope, we were saved. But hope that is seen is no hope at all. Who hopes for what they already have?

Hope is confidence in the unseen. However, if hope is unseen, how can we truly fully trust it? Throughout our day, we have learned to trust the couch we sit on or the toothbrush we brush our teeth with as we can physically "see" it. Alternatively, did you realize that there are many things in life that we have learned to trust without seeing? For example, we can trust that baking cinnamon buns in the oven will leave a delicious aroma in our home and that our insurance company will cover a certain amount of loss incurred. We are fully confident in them as these are legal and natural laws. Similarly, although we can't see it, we can be full of hope. Hope assures us that we can be confident in it because it's the law of God.

"Now faith is confidence in what we hope for and assurance about what we do not see."

Hope Follows Trust

When we build healthy relationship with ourselves, with God our creator and others, we foster trust to share circumstances that are near and dear to our hearts. Trust produces obedience, which produces overflowing hope, which results in greater joy, love and peace for all.

The Gift of Hope

Hope given by Him works together to give us confidence, joy, peace, power and love. Hope is a gift. Hope does not put us to shame because God's unconditional, infinite love he has for us all has been poured out into our hearts.

Hope Endures

Hoping in God will never lead us astray as He has a greater plan and unique purpose for each one of us, a future that is full of hope. *"There is surely a future hope for you, and your hope will not be cut off."*

Hope is Being in Service to Others

Let us hold unswervingly to the hope we profess, for he who promised is faithful. And let us consider how we may spur one another on toward love and good deeds, …

The Present and Future of Hope: Why Sharing Stories of Hope Matters

When you share your story of Hope in the present with others, you can bring about healing and greater hope not only in your own life but also bring healing and inspire positivity and greater purpose for many others. Perhaps your story might even save a life by letting someone know through the sharing of your personal experience that they are loved, a valued member of society and are not alone.

Have you ever thought to stop and think that the majority of us, regardless of age, background or geographic location, are consistently surrounded by stories each day? Whether we think about our lives in terms of stories or not, we are being shaped by them in more profound ways than one.

The focus and purpose of the writing of this book are to share many incredible stories of Hope with you here today to spark a ray of light and bring about hopeful possibilities within a community that truly cares deeply about your well-being. This emphasis on storytelling comes from many awe-inspiring personal experiences and moments I had growing up with my grandparents and many others who would share many stories from long ago that seemed to be almost out of this world. No matter what, though, it was these stories that united us together to trust and support one another in community.

Stories are an extremely powerful action-inspired way of communicating ideas; they highlight our experiences, make sense of what we know, and create a synergistic flow of continuity. We individually learn by both hearing and telling stories and also by practising through being an integral part of the stories themselves. Non-coincidentally, some of the greatest educators, speakers, change-makers and leaders in our world have developed and honed in on the art of storytelling as a way to inspire and bring hope to the masses. In the increasingly chaotic, destructive world we live in, we need now more desperately than ever before to hear and share more hopeful stories of the tremendous amount of good and miraculous encounters that happen in our world every moment of every day. It is like a good ripple of HOPE that is used through stories to help other people elevate one step at a time. This is where great things are brought to fruition, and compounded accomplishments happen over time.

It is through stories that we understand who we are and teach others about what they ought to be and can be. Through stories, we learn many valuable life lessons and pass this historical wisdom and higher knowledge on to the next generation. They ultimately connect us to our past while also giving us the clarity required to guide our future forward in fruitful ways through learning how to be mindful in the present moment.

The Power of Prayer: Hope and Healing By Nadene Joy

Prayer is the heart of hope. Prayer can be an expression of greater love and hope which is a way of affirming our deeply embedded core values and of connecting with God. For example, prayers for those who are sick are a way of expressing solidarity with the sufferer and hope for healing and recovery. Prayer that inspires, fills us with hope, and gives us the courage to face tragedy and disaster, will ultimately guide and lead us to actively seek aligned solutions to move us towards action to turn our dreams into reality. Such prayer when spoken either silently or preferably aloud with dominion, conviction and authority from the heart is genuine, authentic, never vain and is real and moves us towards eternal infinite trust and surrender graciously towards and into a deeper connection with self and God as our ultimate rock, solid foundation for all, our eternally loving, omnipresent and magnificent Lord and Saviour. People often feel discouraged when they feel they have incessantly lost a connection with God or feel that they've ultimately failed to live up to the potential granted to them. The untapped potential lives deeply in our soul and becomes one of the greatest regrets of the dying in their death bed. It is not what they have done, but rather what they didn't do that leaves the greatest hole in their soul. The what if's of life forever haunt their existence. Know that each one of you are given a heart of courage and that God will never put you in a situation he knows you can't handle. All things work for the good of those who love Him. There's no such thing as good or bad as it has been proven time and time again that we grow our character most and learn the greatest soul lessons through the tribulations, struggles and most difficult times. It us through these difficult times we learn to completely surrender and trust Gods divinely orchestrates plan over our own earthly agendas or expectations or desires of the flesh. It us also most times during our struggles where our destiny and purpose is born so we can help transform others lives who are struggling with similar life experiences as what we have gone though. There are no coincidences in life as every experience, every person, every success and every disappointment has been planned and perfectly laid out since the day you were conceived in your mothers womb. You are invited, in this present moment, to move past all and let go of the numerous disappointments from the past towards greater unconditional love, forgiveness and acceptance of self and of all others who have hurt or wronged you in anyway. The present moment is all we truly have as the past has already happened and there's nothing we can do to ever change this and the future has not yet taken place so there is no point in worrying about something that hasn't already happened. The peace and hope we long for comes from a higher knowing and believing in the present moment and taking positive actions forward starting now according to Gods guidance. Without prayer and meditation to hear Gods whispers in our heart and divine guidance and in addition, without the courage given to us to take actions towards living out our wildest dreams, Hope becomes just a dream or thought in our minds and will not be manifested into physical form and reality. No matter how hard you try and hope for something, if you just "think" about it all day and do not "do" anything to move towards it, it will stay just that, a dream. Hope with action is like fire with fuel. Action fuels Hope and solemnly begins with prayer from the heart. When you pray, it is a relationship and real communication between you and God. He knows you deeply and loves you fully. When you feel alone and like the pain of your circumstance or life is too much to bear and can't talk to anyone about a discouragement in your life or faith, God will always be there to listen, just as He is there to infinitely celebrate successes and the happier joyful times in life. Did you know that the number one limiting belief in the world in "I am not good enough?" Feelings that you're not good enough and holding onto faults and failings lend themselves lead to a spiritual discouragement can be extremely difficult to overcome. This is where a consistent daily prayerful and meditative practice can help. We all have felt discouraged, like giving up and like we are stuck in a current situation. Many different situations and emotions can quickly lead us into a downward spiral when we don't have the support, tools or perspective to face them head on. Life in general, relationships, work, finances, family, friends and health can all become instrumental catalysts for our many discouragements and disappointments we experience in everyday life and can manifest themselves in feelings such as: * Hopelessness * Grief * Shame/Guilt * Failure * Uncertainty * Anger The good news is that, with greater awareness comes change and while there are countless causes of spiritual discouragement, how we react, respond and address them from the inside out is tried and true. For example, If someone has ever said or did something triggered you to feel a negative response in anyway such as teaching with anger and lashing out or feeling envious or jealous just to name a few, know this is one of the greatest blessings you can receive and is a blessing and not a curse and those people are mirrors to you and what you haven't let go of and heal from your past that you may have been consciously unaware of previously. When you feel "triggered" in anyway know that it is a perfect opportunity to look within your heart and go into prayer and meditation asking God to show you what you need to let go of or to show you the unhealthy toxic memory or memories that you have been holding onto that is now ready to be healed once and for all to bring you towards discovering more about who you truly are as it removes the barriers that have been preventing you from seeing yourself and who you truly are with clarity before society, family, parents, teachers etc protected their beliefs onto you. It is important to pray to forgive all others who have hurt you in anyway and don't forget to also pray for forgiveness and unconditional love towards yourself and the poor decisions you have made and also for l others you may have hurt along the way. With complete awareness, forgiveness and unconditional love comes freedom, greater hope, healing and peace for all. In addition, we can approach our difficult times and this discouragement by removing fear buy not giving it any attention and by creating a safe space by bringing your feelings from the depths of your wounded heart before God. Completely turn to God through prayer and dare to be completely vulnerable to open your heart to Him for him to completely restore it back to unconditional love. It can be a scary thought at first to be completely vulnerable with God, and others we fully trust, but I promise you that what awaits on the other side is well worth the effort and is so incomprehensible to the human mind of suffering in a good way to move towards complete freedom, healing and grace. When you completely surrender all, be ready and with expectant prayer to expect the unexpected. Consistent prayer from the heart also releases the extraordinary power of God's blessing and healing on your life and circumstances. I have personally witnessed the healing power of the Holy Spirit firsthand on thousands of people of all ages, all geographic locations and status across the globe. We have hope because we know God always hears our prayers. Just knowing we are never alone gives us hope. Prayers never go unheard and are always answered for the higher good of yourself and that of all of humanity. When your prayers, goals and dreams are aligned with your higher morals and values and those of Godly principles based around love, peace, faith, joy, kindness to all, magical things happen. We must recognize that in order to achieve our goals, desires and complete health that with man and the flesh alone this is important impossible, but with the will of God All things are possible. When we pray and meditate daily, prayer leads us towards greater hope, love, healing and peace through actions divinely orchestrated by God which are courageously taken throughout our journey of life. We have "Eternal Hope" in God versus "Worldly Hope" because it is impossible for God to lie. He is the ultimate reliable source of hope and perfection. His changeless consistent reliable character is the foundation of all of his promises. Whatever he says he will do is as good as done, and when we hope in his promises, this hope becomes an anchor for the soul, both firm and secure. Pray with complete expectancy, know it is already done and have grace and compassion and complete acceptance for yourself no all others you come across as you never know what they are going through. Know there are truly no coincidences in life and that you are exactly where you are meant to be on your journey of becoming the best version of yourself and person of character you can be and are continuously moving towards infinitely unleashing and untapping your full God-given potential, unique gifts and talents and purpose in life to also positively impact many others along the way! *"Rejoice in hope, be patient in tribulation, be constant in prayer."*

Mr. Junaid Kaiser from Pakistan, states that for many, prayer gives comfort, guidance, and a sense of connection to a greater divine power. It also provides a sense of hope and optimism. It helps to reduce stress and promote feelings of calm and inner peace. Some studies have suggested that prayer may have positive effects on physical and mental health. Surely, prayers can provide hope to individuals who engage in them. This can be a source of comfort and encouragement, especially during times of hardship or uncertainty. Prayers can also provide a sense of purpose and meaning, helping individuals to feel that they are part of something larger than their own individual lives. This can be particularly important for people who are struggling with feelings of isolation or loneliness. There are many holy verses from various religious traditions that can provide inspiration and hope to those who pray: From the Christian Bible: "*May the God of hope fill you with all joy and peace as you trust in him, so that you may overflow with hope by the power of the Holy Spirit.*" - Romans 15:13 From the Quran (Islamic scripture): "*And seek help through patience and prayer, and indeed, it is difficult except for the humbly submissive [to Allah]*" - Surah Al-Baqarah 2:45 From the Hebrew Bible: "*The Lord is my strength and my shield; my heart trusts in him, and he helps me. My heart leaps for joy, and with my song I praise him.*" - Psalm 28:7 From the Bhagavad Gita (Hindu scripture): "*Let a man lift himself by his own self alone, let him not lower himself; his self alone is his friend, his self alone is his enemy.*" - Bhagavad Gita 6:5 These verses, and many others like them, can provide comfort, guidance, and hope to those who pray and seek inspiration from religious texts. The Biblical verses that speak to the power of prayers: "*Therefore I tell you, whatever you ask for in prayer, believe that you have received it, and it will be yours.*" - Mark 11:24 "*Do not be anxious about anything, but in every situation, by prayer and petition, with thanksgiving, present your requests to God.*" - Philippians 4:6 "*If my people, who are called by my name, will humble themselves and pray and seek my face and turn from their wicked ways, then I will hear from heaven, and I will forgive their sin and will heal their land.*" - 2 Chronicles 7:14 "*And pray in the Spirit on all occasions with all kinds of prayers and requests. With this in mind, be alert and always keep on praying for all the Lord's people.*" - Ephesians 6:18 These verses, and others like them, emphasize the importance of prayer as a means of connecting with God and seeking guidance, comfort, and blessings. They also emphasize the importance of faith and trust in God's power and ability to answer prayer. Verses in the Bible that offer hope to those who are facing difficult situations: *"For I know the plans I have for you,"* declares the Lord, *"plans to prosper you and not to harm you, plans to give you hope and a future."* - Jeremiah 29:11 *"May the God of hope fill you with all joy and peace as you trust in him, so that you may overflow with hope by the power of the Holy Spirit."* - Romans 15:13 *"He heals the brokenhearted and binds up their wounds."* - Psalm 147:3 *"Even though I walk through the darkest valley, I will fear no evil, for you are with me; your rod and your staff, they comfort me."* - Psalm 23:4 These verses, and many others like them, offer comfort, encouragement, and assurance to those who are facing difficult circumstances. They remind us of God's love, mercy, and faithfulness, and the hope we can find in Him through completely trusting and surrendering to His perfectly divinely orchestrated plan and purpose for our life, which starts with quest reflection through prayer which leads to greater guidance and clarity from God on what specific steps and actions to take. No matter what we do and what struggles we are going through, prayer is our solid foundation and rock in which, through God alone, all things are possible!

Stories heal.
We need stories to better understand our identity, dignity, worth, and ultimately our place in the world.

STORIES OF HOPE FROM AROUND THE WORLD
By Aliza Ansari

THE ART OF LEARNING LIFE

Life is not a one-way road; rather, it is a two-way road with unforeseen speed breakers, pits, and varied speed ranges. When we are growing up and are in our transformational years, we are often taught that it is going to be a linear path with some basic steps to complete in the pursuit of glory. We tell our young ones what will happen after we get educated, have stable careers, a marriage, some kids, and a big house. However, the biggest mistake we make is that we do not tell our children what to do if things don't turn out as planned and how to react if met with failure. Over a few years, I realized that the indoctrination that stresses leading a 'perfect life' is so deeply ingrained in every one of us that there has been no room left to input the ideals to act upon if there are obstacles, hindrances, or temporary failures. This is why most people in this world feel lost and abandoned and self-collapse when met with tragedies of life because they were never educated on how to collect themselves in moments of despair and dejection. Failures and obstacles are the inexorable realities of our lives, but we do not treat them the same as we deal with our victories, celebrations, and triumphs. Dealing with a hard time in life is what defines our true character because it is these testing times that bring out the best in us and train us to be stronger and more resilient in the future. Often the most powerful figures in the world are those who have endured their pernicious times with the utmost strength and resilience. Some of the most common denominators of a person's innate courage are their behaviour when things are not in their favour, their reaction to adversity and their motivation not to give up.

Those who successfully pass hardships with their heads held high are the ones who're doing something good in life because mastering skills of living a great life is an exclusive art that comes with constant learning, determination, and the urge to become a better version of yourself.

Growing up, my father had been my biggest inspiration to work hard, lead an independent life and be a headstrong person. Coming from an influential and wealthy family, my father had a career laid down for him, but instead, he chose to carve out one for himself through his own abilities, talent, and passion. He has instilled the same set of values and teachings in me, to follow my dreams, work harder if required and trust myself and my abilities above anything else.

To have a plan-B in life can have extremely successful results. To know where we stand if our primary plan stumbles is not just a good strategic plan but also serves as a comforting trampoline to land on and bounce back, with more force to achieve the set target even better.

A lot of times, people wear horse-blinders in life while chasing perfection, which leads them to miss the process of achieving it. The minor lessons and the subtle teachings that are part and parcel of their journey are often overlooked and neglected. Often, the biggest lessons of life are hidden in those journeys we take to achieve our goals and destination. The nitty-gritty of the pain we endure in doing so, the challenges we face, and the lessons we learn from them are lost.

How you approach your life speaks volumes about yourself.

A lot of humans are content in passively coasting along and letting life take the lead in hopes of landing on their desired shore, while others make active choices to understand themselves, their needs and their passion and steer the wheel of their 'lifeboat' to their ultimate destination.

Some golden rules in life that define our paths are as follows:

1: Think about and create your realities. Your thoughts have the power to shape your life; whatever you fixate on ultimately becomes your reality. Surrounding your mind with positive and mindful thoughts will project illuminative effects on what reaches you in life.

2: Don't let outside fears shake your inner confidence. The lesser heed your pay to the external noise, the nearer you get to reaching your goals.

3: A good reputation is the greatest asset you have. It will pay off in dividends forever and will never devalue. Your reputation, which is built on the foundation of your character entails the words you speak and the actions you take. Having a strong character, solid values and high-vibrational demeanour will never let you down.

4: You are never over until you decide to be. Negativity is very powerful and can cause premature death. Refrain from using words like 'I can't ever accomplish anything' as these are self-inflicted failures that welcome friction, jolts and much unnecessary resistance in life.

5: Don't let your success get to your head. Being humble is a virtue that keeps us grounded and reminds us of our imperfections as humans. It not only brings humility but also creates room for improvement and new learning.

I believe as young professionals, our first and foremost duty is to inculcate these traits in ourselves before we preach these to others. Our aura should radiate our mindsets. Nothing is more attractive than a mindful soul who knows how to excel at life against all odds.

One word of inspiration I choose to share is "Perseverance."

I personally chose this word as Perseverance is the key to unlocking all glory. The essence of its value is to remember that it will always pay off twice what is invested.

"Live your life in such a way that tomorrow when you look back on the journey, the biggest wrinkle that covers your face is a smile denoting fulfilment, gratification and tranquillity." -Aliza Ansari

Aliza Ansari

Aliza Ansari is a 24-year-old woman who is a software engineer by profession and a humanitarian. by heart. She was born and raised in Karachi, Pakistan. Although she graduated in 2021 with a high GPA of 3.4 and landed a promising career, she has always felt that her real purpose goes far beyond that. Being the voice of the voiceless brings tranquillity and joy to her soul. She feels our true sense of self comes from distributing our light with the intent to cut through the darkness that surrounds our world. As the official Youth Ambassador of the Global Movement of Hope, she pledges to do her bit to be the light at the end of the tunnel for those who have no one to turn to and to bring trust, enlightenment, hope and the ability to dream again to a neglected part of the human family.

Aliza Ansari

LinkedIn: www.linkedin.com/in/aliza-ansari

Email: aliza5aliza@gmail.com

Hope

By Carmel Bell M.I

When I think of Hope, the phrase 'on a wing and a prayer' comes to mind. Hope is what we feel when we desire a certain outcome. But Hope can be far more profound, far more than a feel-good emotion. Hope is the substance that lies buried deep inside; it keeps you going when nothing else will. Hope is the travelling companion we all need when we are facing an uncertain but critical outcome.Hope, accessible by thought, prayer, or sometimes tears of joy or grief, is the feeling that I personally have drawn on when I have faced tough odds and was unsure if I had the courage, resilience or will to endure.There have been moments in my life when no hope felt possible, but I dug down and found that spark deep within. I believe we all know that feeling and that place. Without its presence, too many turn to other options that will permanently remove hope.In moments of extreme despair, I have accessed it by speaking to the Source/God.

I remember when I was a child, prayer was expected, and it was a duty, not a joy. But hope, when expressed with joy, is the stuff that enhances your ability to cope. Hope will strengthen the coping ability and improve the quality of life, even in those with chronic or incurable illnesses.

Equally, a lack of hope is associated with depression and anxiety, which will negatively impact the quality of life.There have been times when I have had no idea what has kept me going, and yet, something encouraged me, and inspired me to keep moving forward. That has been Hope. Profound Hope — because that feeling could only be Hope. Sometimes foolish, sometimes warranted, it encompasses both strength and courage. It draws on resilience and even the deepest wells of grief. It brings forth the battle cry, 'Once more into the fray!'

Armed with such belief in yourself, hope is the cousin of faith and the friend of belief.

It is so easy to relegate it to the realms of minor wishes; it is more necessary to life than we give it credit for. Hope inspires the deep core strength to know that against all odds, you have a chance to succeed.What would life be without hope? It would be darkness and despair.There have been moments when I have lost all hope, when I have found myself on my knees, crying, when the pain of breathing has been impossible to bear. I had no hope that what I needed to achieve or heal could be done. And then, from out of the dark, has come the unexpected wave of hope.

And that has been enough to keep me going.

Whether it be on a wing, or a prayer, without hope, you would have ... no hope of truly Being.

Carmel Bell

Carmel Bell, Conscious Life Creator, is from Melbourne, Australia and is recognized as one of the top ten Medical Intuitives in the world. 10,000 clients have passed through her clinic, while her college attracts many who wish to learn her techniques. She is Vice President of the International Association of Medical Intuitives and founder and president of the Australian branch.

THE LIFE OF JUNNK

By Sam McGowan

Although difficult at times, my journey has been incredible and has opened a completely unique life that I could never have imagined for myself. I've travelled the world, performed for thousands, developed a business, managed franchises, and negotiated with some of the largest entertainment companies, all the while working alongside some of my best friends. Together we embarked on a journey totally unique to us, providing the world with something that previously did not exist, and is one of the most fulfilling aspects of it all. It's no exaggeration to say JunNk has been a complete blessing in my life, full of exciting moments and essential life lessons, providing me with so many wonderful memories and the belief that anything is possible. The road has been long and fun, and I'm excited to share my story with you so far.

At age sixteen, I still didn't know exactly what I wanted to do until I attended college to study Performing Arts. During these two incredible years, I fell in love with performing and knew from that point on it was what I wanted in my future. After leaving college, my plans for performing were somewhat vague, so while I was still discovering precisely what I wanted to do, I started picking up various manual labour jobs, such as Arboriculturist, Builder, Plumber, Electrician and Farm and Plant operator to name a few. This type of work came quite naturally to me, thanks in large part to all those years growing up helping my Dad, who has always been practical and would frequently get me involved in whatever he was doing, whether it was cutting hedges or getting under the bonnet to help him restore a classic car. The skills I learned from my Dad along with all the experience gained from working such a diverse range of practical jobs, became instrumental (pun intended) in what was to come next for me and the journey I have since embarked on.

In 2008 I started something that was going to change my life forever. At this point, it was only a vision, a glimmer of possibility that could eventually become a career of a lifetime. A few of my best friends and I expanded on an idea that originated in college three years earlier, creating a show around percussion and acapella singing. The concept was to use commonly discarded trash items to make music, such as barrels, pipes, buckets, and bottles. The original reasoning behind using these items was very simple; we had no money. Being fresh out of college, we had very few resources, so using things that were being thrown out was the cheapest way to fund our project. The phrase, 'One man's junk is another man's treasure,' was extremely fitting in this case. In addition to being highly cost-effective for us as 'starving artists' trying to get our feet off the ground, the recyclable nature of our instruments instantly gave our show a sustainable, 'green' aspect, a theme that now runs strong through my veins and imprints on everything I do, both within the business and my personal life.

The process of initial ideation to financial fruition would take a few years, and during this time, I continued to work my various labour jobs on the side in order to save and invest money into my passion project. Things were slow, but we kept grinding, and in 2012 something amazing happened. After much hard work, we were fortunate enough to win a TV competition, presenting us with £25k in prize money. The timing could not have been better, as this gave us a huge and much-needed leg up with financial resources for both us as individuals and the company. Riding on the success of our TV show win, JunNk was then booked on a full UK theatre tour. It was very easy in this moment to think that things were really starting to move forward and that we were officially on our way, but of course, the path to success is often far more complicated and eventful than we first expected.

Little did we know that just as we were starting the tour, the very first day in fact, we found out the TV show had been axed, and our tour producer had completely pulled out. We had been stung, and left high and dry with a fully booked, four-month tour that we were contracted to complete. Finding ourselves between a sharp rock and a very hard place, I made the decision to buy everything we needed to complete the tour, meaning £20k split across my credit cards plus drawing on my personal savings. To make matters worse, unfortunately, the marketing for the tour never even started, so right from the start, we were constantly struggling to advertise our shows and sell enough tickets. Unsurprisingly, the tour was a flop. However, although overall, we lost money, we did manage to cover the majority of the costs and most importantly, learned a valuable lesson that set the precedence for how I would continue to operate the business. I learned the importance of making smart choices and being aware of people eager to take advantage of what you've got for their own personal gain. It highlighted that the path toward our goal would not always be straightforward, but we should not give up. Sometimes we're required to swim through cold, murky waters before we get to the warm, crystal-clear oceans. All you've got to do is just keep swimming.

The struggle bus continued its journey along the bumpy road for the next few years as I worked hard to further establish more contacts and pave the journey for JunNk's future. It was a 24/7, 365 commitment, every day rolling out of bed up to my desk to keep the developments going, and I loved it. I was hungry for the work and constantly generating ideas to push the JunNk brand worldwide, the passion and determination making the early mornings and long days easy. Soon the company started working more frequently, which was great, but it also meant I was juggling performing in the group and running the business simultaneously, oscillating between international shows and working from my home office every other week. As popularity and demand continued to grow, I found I was increasingly turning down gigs, which was incredibly frustrating. I worked hard to open these prospects just to say no, and it didn't make sense, ultimately leading me to make a tough decision.

After some careful consideration, I decided to stop performing so that I could focus my attention solely on growing the brand from offstage. I had been performing in the show for the past nine years, and it was one of the things I loved the most. It was the joy of performing that got me to this point, and it was very hard to imagine stopping, but the decision was made easier by remembering some advice once offered to me by a close friend and mentor, *'Begin with the end in mind.'* This quote structures my life and my day-to-day decisions and accurately depicts the exact reason why I decided to step down from the stage. I had a vision of where I wanted JunNk to get to, and achieving this meant sacrificing performing, at least for now. I needed to focus all my energy on growing the show and being able to accept as many jobs as possible, even if that meant I wasn't on them myself. Short-term pain for long-term gain, as some say, and I feel this holds true for anything notable we want to do in our lives. Nothing worthwhile comes easy, and sacrifices often need to be made now so that we may flourish later on.

2018 was a big year, full to the brim with expansion, risk, and turmoil. After replacing myself in the show, I created a second JunNk team in the UK to further meet the growing demand for the show. Despite initially being an exciting new prospect, my resilience was quickly tested yet again, as two weeks before the second team's first three-month tour started, fifty percent of the cast dropped out along with the tour manager/driver. This was not good; however, just like every other time I have faced adversity, I found a way to solve the problem and keep moving forward. When we encounter numerous setbacks, it's all too easy to play the victim and cry out, 'why me?!' but having the ability to keep a cool head in testing moments is a skill that I have developed along this journey. Something that helps me deal with these situations is practising gratitude. So, I take a deep breath, I think about how grateful I am for all the good things in my life, and in that moment, it helps shift my perspective to something positive and ultimately helps me overcome what I need to.

Remarkably, juggling the second team still wasn't enough to fulfil incoming demand, as we were receiving interest from overseas, with our biggest client asking for a team based in the USA. Around the time this was happening, however, I was going through a difficult phase in my personal life, and it was something that would later prove to be my toughest test to date. My eight-year relationship came to a swift end at the exact time my fiancé and I were busy buying our first home. At the time, this was not a decision I wanted, which ultimately left me emotionally drained and feeling mentally lost. I put on a brave face to keep the company moving, as I never wanted it to affect everything that I had worked for. At the risk of falling down an emotional spiral, my friends and family were there to catch me and help me bounce back, helping me rediscover my former self and realize that settling down in the UK wasn't what I truly wanted for my future and that my destiny, and perhaps JunNk's as well, was waiting elsewhere. I had renewed vigour, and so upon receiving my deposit back from the house, I felt I needed to put it towards something positive, something progressive, where I could capitalize on this renewed sense of freedom and infinite possibility. As such, I took the money and decided to fly to the USA and chase the American dream, JunNk style.

Once in America, I collaborated with a production company based in Orlando, Florida, which were incredible in providing me with an excellent foundation to work from. I had a place to stay, a rehearsal space, a workshop, essentially everything I needed to set up 'JunNk USA.' This was an incredibly bold move and was the biggest leap I had taken to date, involving a large number of risks that I honestly hadn't fully accounted for. There was undoubtedly an emotional drive behind this venture, as personally, I was still struggling and despite having positive intentions, I could feel my anguish starting to cloud my normal business reasoning. I knew I had to dig deep, fix up and focus on the tasks at hand, as there was a lot going on at once, and it required my full attention. In addition to setting up the USA group, we had one team busy touring in China while another was flying between cruises in Europe. At the same time I was also working on a completely different production with a company in Dubai, as well as helping cast for a show in Abu Dhabi. I'd be lying if I said that wasn't a lot. However, I remember back to the early years when opportunities were few and far between, and now I find myself frequently being asked to create, develop, write and produce shows, whether that be for JunNk or other companies entirely, and I love it. Sometimes it is a lot on my plate at once, but I always say yes to these opportunities because there was once a time when there were none to say yes to, and I want to continually put myself and the company in the best possible position to grow and progress without limitations.

Things in America continued to move forward, with the USA team performing their first paid shows just a month after they finished training. The coming months would prove to only get busier for both them and the company as a whole, as throughout 2019, we had twenty-four cast members spread across three continents. JunNk was being seen by millions worldwide, and we were building stronger relationships with our client base to secure more full-time contracts. With nearly two years' worth of work secured and more contracts still being added, we were at full strength. The dream was in motion, and the years of hard work and persistence were finally starting to pay off. Then, in the blink of an eye, came 2020, the year that changed the world. As was the case for many others, we lost all our work overnight, and, in that moment it felt like all of our progress went along with it. The wind had truly been taken out of our sails just as we were picking up speed, and I honestly couldn't believe it was happening.

As maddening as it was, it would be all too easy to get upset and frustrated over what the pandemic has taken from myself and from

JunNk. However, in times like these, I feel it's important to remind ourselves of the things that matter most to us, like our health and our family. Dealing with what has probably been the most significant setback of mine and JunNk's entire journey, I realized it was time again to take a breath and focus on what I'm grateful for, to shift my perspective in this scenario and look ahead with positivity. How can I overcome this adversity? I've done it before, and I'll do it again. I took this opportunity to refocus and re-evaluate what it was I wanted, looking at the journey I was on before the pandemic and deciding whether it was making me happy. In this sense, the pandemic ended up being a blessing in disguise, as even though JunNk was constantly growing up until that point, there were a few areas in my life that were falling short, and I realized I was investing too much time in certain projects that ultimately left me drained and unfulfilled. Time is our most valuable currency, and I needed to start spending it more wisely. Having this time to reflect blessed me with a refreshed outlook, allowing me to get clear about what I wanted both my and the company's future to look like. As a result, I have reignited my artistic passion by branching out into writing commercial music in the hope of creating a different opportunity to showcase the unique sounds of JunNk in a totally new way. I have also spent time securing my financial future by creating passive income from real estate investments in the UK, allowing me to earn money while freeing up time to focus on what is most important to me.

Since resuming after the pandemic, JunNk has bounced back very strongly, with the show flourishing on a new path along with many exciting opportunities coming up on the horizon. The journey over the past fifteen years has been a roller coaster ride, involving many ups and downs, twists and turns, and all too often feeling very close to derailing. It hasn't always been easy, but I hope that through my story, people can realize that it's not what happens to us that matters, but how we react and what we do next, and that it's entirely down to us and the outlook we have in any given situation. Being able to shift our perspective and use it to create something better is one of the most powerful traits we have as humans and is a value that I treasure above all else. Having this mindset has therefore allowed me to stay persistent and keep going in the face of adversity, never giving up and continuing to pursue what I really want. I may not necessarily be where I want to be or where I thought I would be at this time, but learning how to adjust my attitude is what has enabled me to keep swimming through those murky waters and still be in one piece, still getting closer and closer to that warm, clear ocean, and never forgetting to enjoy the swim itself.

The word I think most resonates with me in the context of my journey is 'perspective.' To me, being able to shift our perspective is like having a superpower, enabling us to alter our own reality and giving us the opportunity to view the world and any situation in whichever way we choose. This concept is very important to me, as it is this ability that allows us to stay calm and adjust our attitude in the face of adversity, interpret the experience in a positive way and keep moving forward. No matter what happens to us in life, the way we interpret our experiences can have a profound effect on what comes next. When we change our perspective, we change our future, good or bad, and I urge everyone to chase the good.

A quote I frequently refer to that keeps me going along my journey and reminds me of the importance of perspective is simply, 'Success is entirely subjective.' We have all sorts of expectations thrust upon us from the moment we're born, over time increasing the pressure from all around us to do and be certain things by a certain age. This quote reminds me that we are the ones in control of our own lives and that contrary to society's expectations, success can mean whatever we want it to. We can do and be anything we desire and must always have the courage to stand in our truth and live life on our own terms. Dream big, work hard, and don't for a second live according to anyone else's expectations. This is your life, so live it for you!

Sam McGowan

Sam McGowan is the founder and CEO of the award-winning show, JunNk; a comedy-percussion group that uses common junkyard items to produce an entertaining and innovative musical experience. His talent for both performing and business has helped make JunNk an international phenomenon, with the show entertaining millions of people around the world for the past ten years. During this time, the group has successfully performed for countless big-name companies, with the show being featured on various cruise lines such as Disney, Norwegian, Celebrity, Royal Caribbean, and P&O, as well as completing multiple theatre tours in China, headlining large European music festivals, and attending an array of high-end corporate events worldwide. JunNk has won many awards over the years, most notably Event Awards' Act of the Year, Best Family Show at Orlando Fringe and Spirit of the Fringe at The Edinburgh Festival, as well as being crowned TV's Don't Stop Me Now competition winners. The show has also been featured on multiple international media outlets, including BBC, ITV and SKY ONE in the UK, and FOX 35 in the U.S.A.

Sam is a multi-talented individual, and in addition to his success with JunNk wears many hats while involving himself with other artistic endeavours. Such roles include creative director, manager, producer, multi-instrumentalist, songwriter, music producer, videographer, and editor. Having received recognition for his extraordinary creative ability, he was hand-picked to assist leading creatives with producing different shows using his unique JunNk experience, developing bespoke instruments from unconventional items while working alongside entertainment giants such as Warner Bro's, Ferrari, and Disney.

In addition to his creative flare, Sam's excellent aptitude for business has enabled him to take JunNk from its humble beginnings and expand it into an internationally-franchised company, running multiple teams and managing numerous cast members simultaneously.

He is a compassionate leader with a warm personality and positive attitude that feeds into everything he does. An avid surfer and keen traveller, Sam also has an inspiring zest for life, constantly eager to maximize every opportunity that comes his way and provide as much value to all those around him.

Sam McGowan

www.JunNk.co.uk

Sam@JunNk.co.uk

LinkedIn:www.linkedin.com/in/sam-mcgowan-589a976b

STOP SETTLING – ANSWER YOUR CALLING AND OVERCOME OBSTACLES!

By Meera Shah

This is a story about how Meera Shah overcame a difficult period in her life during the Covid Pandemic and answered the calling to get up and move forward. One she wishes to share with you and inspire you to take the journey when you feel called.

Have you ever been unhappy in a job – the one you know you have outgrown quite a while ago, but you convince yourself to stay there? You tell yourself that you need the stability or the money, or perhaps now is not the right time to move, or you don't know what to do next. And then you even convince yourself that it's not that bad. Yet you know deep down in your heart that you want more.

And then boom! There's a restructuring or some external event, and the company makes you redundant.

Two emotions immediately come to the surface. Firstly, relief as the decision you needed to make has been made for you, and you feel free. But then a second emotion rises where you are really annoyed as they have terminated your contract.

This has happened to me a few times in my life – the last one just before the Pandemic in 2019.

I live in London, England, and I used to work in the high-profile financial sector as a banker and consultant. However, my true passion has always been in personal development, wanting to help others reach their highest potential and live their dream.

In 2019, I was working on a consulting assignment in the banking sector – one I had done many times before and I knew I had outgrown. However, I kept telling myself I needed the money and the stability, and I wasn't ready yet to give it all up.

This was my life at the time:

Monday to Friday: Work, gym, eat, relax, repeat

Saturday – Sunday: Chores, relax, socialize, and get ready for Monday.

I was always blue on a Sunday – I knew the term Sunday blues all too well. In fact, mine would start way earlier – they would start on Sunday afternoon when I decided I couldn't have a nap as it would mess up my sleep that night.

Eventually, late in 2019, I completed my assignment, and the company didn't renew me for a new piece of work as they didn't have the budget.

Boom.

Phase 1 – The Calling

This is what I term as the first phase in a transformation journey: THE CALLING. The calling can be an internal thing which is often a choice (wanting more, outgrown something, being unhappy), or it can be an external thing which becomes a forced situation (economy, redundancy, illness, etc.). The calling is essentially a strong desire or a forced need to change – step 1 of the transformation journey.

We go through several transformations in our life. Every time we outgrow something or start a new phase, we embark on a transformation. Oftentimes, this is unconscious rather than conscious.

The benefits of doing this consciously are that you know exactly what you are doing, why you are doing it and the effort required. It stops you from giving up and it really helps you to focus your energy on the right things. Once we decide to answer the calling - Step 2 of the journey follows – the commitment.

In my example, once my contract was not renewed, I went into my usual mode and started looking for new contracts. However, the Pandemic hit – and I couldn't get another contract. This forced me to pause and take a hard look and think about what to do next.

I knew this was my chance to do something different. I deliberated for a long time even though in my heart, I knew what I wanted to do. I had dreamt of becoming a coach and had planted the seeds (reading, training, raising my skills, and taking seminars) a long, long time ago. Was it time to step into it?

Phase 2 – Commitment

The Pandemic hugely exacerbated the fears on the planet on so many levels - health, loneliness, and economic – and I was not spared. It was the worst time to be alone and without a job. The fear did get hold of me, and I suffered from anxiety and health issues. I lost hair (really huge bald patches) and ended up with a frozen shoulder – and if you have ever had one, you will know it is one of the most painful, excruciating things you can have.

To make matters worse, I was visiting my family in Kenya when I got Covid. I was feeling very poorly and was really scared as I had really severe symptoms. This was until I realized that I had passed it on to my mum, the one person my family was trying to protect, as she has a lot of underlying conditions. I spent ten days looking after her in isolation, followed by another 14 days with her locked up in a hospital room.

This was a really useful wake-up call for me and got me into action. Suddenly, my own fears and how I was feeling didn't matter. I was so focused on her recovery, as we didn't know if she would make it, that the things that were bothering me – such as feeling ill and scared myself or not being able to sleep properly didn't matter.

This was a big transformation moment for me – one where I found a resiliency I didn't even know I had. I found it and decided that life was very precious, and I was strong enough to get up and engage in it.

Most people I know were impacted by the Covid Pandemic in one way or another. Was there anything in the Pandemic that you learned, or was asking you to look at things differently or make some changes? Did you decide to answer that call?

I knew finally that this was my chance to let go of my lifeboat (the banking) that was keeping me safe but also unhappy and stuck - and fully commit to the thing I was already doing and was really passionate about –personal development. The fear kept holding me back, and in that moment of sitting in the hospital with my mum, wondering if she would make it - I knew it was time to let the fear go.

I was finally ready to commit to my dream. I committed - I was going to do this no matter what it took or how long it took!

Phase 3 - Goal

This is the next phase in the journey. Once you decide to commit, it is essential to set some goals to make it concrete and help you to prioritize your time and energy. I suggest setting small and big goals. Set yourself some small wins to get your momentum and set yourself up for lasting success; then, the big wins become easier.

My big goal was to get back on my feet and set up a thriving business around my dream of coaching, motivating and personal development. I felt it was my purpose – something I was very passionate about and with which I was aligned. I was no longer willing to settle.

But first, I started with the smaller yet equally important goals. They were ones that I could believe in and achieve.

My first goals were to get healthy and get into better sleeping habits. I was so ashamed of my life at that time that I had retreated and had really let myself go. I had put on weight and literally was spending all my time in jogging pants in front of the TV. I needed to change my energy and the way that I felt and looked.

I also wanted to change my mindset as I had got myself into depression and some real anxiety and negativity. Finally, I wanted to stop being ashamed and start socializing again.

I knew I needed these goals achieved before I could attempt the big business one.

Phase 4 – Massive Growth

This is where we deconstruct our old life and start building the new – and it is the easiest place to give up as it takes the longest amount of grit, time and perseverance. However, the rewards are completely worth it as you get to live the life you dream of. If you look at anyone successful, they will tell you how much of this they have done to become successful. Thus it is important to deconstruct unhelpful habits and thoughts and to connect with new thoughts and create new habits. This often involves connecting with new people too.

I suggest starting with one thing. In my case, I decided I was going to give up being negative and thinking I was unlucky and that it wasn't going to work out. I wasn't going to give up. A new mindset I had to cultivate was one of faith, belief and commitment. I also knew I was going to have to work hard to make it work. I was willing to do all of this.

I started eating better, exercising and making a big effort when I dressed up. I made sure I walked every single day in nature, being outside for at least an hour – starting small and building up to 10,000 steps a day. There were some days I would go to the park near my house, and then I had to sit down on a bench as my anxiety would kick in. But slowly, I forced myself to walk, five more minutes, ten more minutes – till I eventually built it up to 10,000 steps.

For anyone interested, there is a really famous healing pilgrimage walk in Spain called the Camino de Santiago. It's a 500-mile walk, and you end up in a gorgeous church where legend has it that the remains of the Apostle Saint James the Great are buried here. The saying on the Camino is ... "Walk it out." Whatever you are feeling - tired, blisters, emotional – walk it out, and the walking will heal it. I really believe this is true, and the Camino is on my bucket list to walk. Ironically, my brother walked it in 2021 and has shared his experiences with me – which has made me want to do it more. He bought me a beautiful shell from the church, and on the back, it reads, "Keep walking; it's your Camino." It's so beautiful, I've kept it on my altar at home. Every time I touch this shell, I literally get emotional and very teary.

Coming back to my time of growth - I prayed every single day and renewed my faith daily – something I still do. I also started waking up earlier – there really is something magical and precious about getting up very early and starting your day. No wonder there are so many books on this. And this was a big one for me - I reduced my TV time to about 3 hours a week from 3 hours a day. I went back to something I had not done in years, reading.

I did something I have now coined as the three Ps: Positivity, Perseverance and Practice. These are not always easy, and it's easy to slip back – but if you do, as soon as you realize you have slipped back, you pick up again. It does eventually get easier and become a habit.

All of this combined made a really big difference in my life. I started to have more faith, felt and looked better and I wanted to engage with life and people. I started to feel like it was going to be possible to turn my life around.

I finally had three things: HOPE, FAITH AND

DETERMINATION.

Phase 5 – WINS

It took a few months, but after putting all the above into practice, I finally started to see some changes, and things started shifting. The daily walks in fresh air and sunlight slowly started lifting my mood. I even started to listen to fun music and dance at home – something I only do when I feel good.

I lost some weight, and I started to see friends again. It made me feel so good – and I realized I was not alone. In fact, I realized that despite all the shame I was feeling, no one else thought of me or saw me in that same way at all.

Fast forward a few months - I managed to do a TEDx talk, my business got nominated for a top 100 business award, I was helping clients, and I started speaking and training in various organizations. Emotionally, I gave up watching TV, which freed up so much time for me. I didn't realize how much time and energy TV was consuming in my life. I started waking up early (there really is a lot of truth in creating that miracle morning). I continue to wake up early. Sometimes I find that I have gone back to my old habits of waking up later or eating unhealthy – but each time, it's quicker and takes less effort to get back to the good habits.

As I continue on my path, there are some things I know have been my pillars and will continue to always be so. I know the path will get rocky at some point, and I might fall again - but I also know that I have my pillars to help me get back up again. Find your pillars that will get you up no matter what. Try and make these into daily habits, an essential part of your day. Some of my pillars are: walking, reading, music, prayer, faith, positivity and taking small actions toward my goal. My sister is also a pillar in my life - I can call on her in any crisis, and she will be there. Do you have someone you can call on? These daily habits will keep you moving forward, even when it doesn't feel like it.

From my mindset of despair and not knowing if this was going to work out, I now know (and have experienced) that it will. When you face this, know yours will too.

I would like to leave you with these top three reflections:

1) This saying (borrowed from the Camino that I deeply resonate with):

"WALK IT OUT." Whatever you are feeling, however you are feeling, keep walking. As the sun sets, so it shall rise again. Personally, I have not walked the Camino yet, but I have seen the stories of many who have. And one day, I definitely will walk it. In my own life, I have witnessed how walking has changed everything. When I am home stressing, I go for a long walk in nature. By the time I come back, my energy has completely changed, nature and light have healed me, I am calm, and I am no longer stressed. I feel completely supported. Sometimes I even want to stay out longer, and I do.

2) What in your life is calling you to change? I invite you to stop settling or let someone else answer that call for you - answer that call for yourself.

3) A famous Henry Ford quote, *"Whether you think you can, or you think you can't – you're right,"* emphasizes how much attitude determines success or failure.

Meera Shah

Meera Shah is a Transformation and Success Coach who grew up in a large, joint family in Nairobi, Kenya. She was shy as a child, which she always wanted to overcome - and this has led her to a passion for personal development since she was young. After qualifying as an accountant, she left Kenya to live in the vibrant big city of London, where she became a successful banker. Meera then went on to do her MBA in London at Bayes Business School and, at the same time, carried on training in all things personal development related. She is now pursuing her passion by applying all the different things she has learned and experienced to help others to be their best and achieve their dreams. When time permits, Meera loves to travel, exploring high+energy places and watching beautiful sunsets all around the world. She is also a thought leader, trainer and speaker (including TEDx) and wants to help improve the mindsets and potential of all humans around the globe.

Meera Shah

www.unlimitedtransformations.com

IG: @meerashahunlimited

Email: meera@unlimitedtransformations.com

Linkedin:www.linkedin.com/in/meerashahunlimited/

www.facebook.com/TheMeeraShah/

My Story of Hope

By Brian Schulman

It was the afternoon of January 2018, my daughter's senior year in High School (now a Junior in College). I'm sitting in my home office.

Not a single white space on the walls is visible as they are plastered with paintings my two kids (aka my Monkeys) had made over the years. She walks into the room, looks at me, and hands me a few pieces of paper.

Standing there, she then sits down in the chair next to me, silent, still looking at me, her eyes signalling me to read what she had put in my hands at that moment.

She wanted to sit with me while I read. I stopped what I was doing and began to read "4 Way Speech Contest Essay ... entitled *Live To Inspire*".

4 WAY SPEECH CONTEST ESSAY

Braeden Shulman

Mrs. Rienick

Period 3

17 January 2018

LIVE TO INSPIRE

This story about to be told is about an extraordinary man, now 42 years young, who accepted all the obstacles life had to throw at him. Now, I know you may be thinking that everyone has different obstacles they just overcome throughout their lifetime, so how is he different from you and me? What makes this particular man different from you and me is the tactic he used when faced with these obstacles. What makes him different from you and me is that he took these obstacles and used them to help make a difference and inspire others never to let life get in the way of their greatness and achievements. What makes us different from everyone else is not the obstacles life throws at us but what we do when faced with these obstacles. Will you choose to accept defeat or choose to persevere?

On May 13, 1975, a child was born in Cedars-Sinai Medical Center in Los Angeles. This child was born three months early, weighing 1 ½ pounds, and because of this, was a premature baby. During the early 80s, he was diagnosed with Tourette Syndrome, which is a kind of tic (involuntary, repetitive movements and vocalization) disorder. One day at camp, the counsellor had to take this young boy to a payphone, tears streaming down his face, to call his mother because his neck was constantly snapping to one side over and over again. He went to various doctors who performed countless medical examinations to try to find a cure for his disorder. Every doctor said the same thing: he is fine; he will grow out of it. One day, in fifth grade, he stood up in front of his entire class and shared with them what Tourette Syndrome was and what living with Tourette Syndrome was like. A huge weight was lifted off his shoulders once he shared his story with his classmates, and it generated many supporters, whether they were friends, parents or teachers. Finally, a specialist at UCLA told him that he would never be able to get rid of this disorder alone and suggested that he take a special drug called Clonidine to help with the tics. Unfortunately, with the drug came horrible side effects. He made a conscious decision not to take the pills and tried to master his condition through focus and determination. After a while, the tics started to diminish and eventually went away completely. No one knows what life has in store for them. All we can do is live until we are forced to face an obstacle in which we must make a choice to either overcome or accept defeat.

The Rotary 4 Way Test demonstrates how one person can make a difference in the lives of others. With the experiences this boy had to face came a life lesson: with determination, perseverance, and support from others, anything can happen. Now at 42 years young, this man chooses to use his story to make a difference in others' lives by inspiring people in times of uncertainty. He implements the Rotary's motto: "Service Before Self," by finding the light in those who cannot find it in themselves, supporting them through their tough obstacles. He helps lift people's spirits in times of hopelessness and despair. He helps people turn their ideas and dreams into realities. He helps build people from the ground up in hopes that they, too, will one day share their stories with others. He makes a difference in this world each and every day, which inspires others to make a difference as well.

Who, may you ask, is this man? Well, he is my father. Out of all the lives he has made a difference in, I believe he made the biggest difference in mine. He inspires me to never give up on what I believe in, to always do what makes me happy, but most importantly, to always live every day as if it were the last because we are never guaranteed a tomorrow. As Gandhi once said, "Be the change you wish to see in the world." Making a difference in the lives of others is my dad's change. What will yours be?

To say I was completely taken aback is an understatement. My eyes looked like Niagara Falls, as I had been bawling while reading.

I never knew that she felt this way about me. She sat on my lap, we hugged, and cried together. My heart smiled with pride as her Dad.

So, now that you've heard my story through the heart of my daughter. There's a question that I get a lot. Almost daily. "How can you be so happy and positive all the time? How do you do it?!"

Coming from where I have, fighting for every breath to make it into the world as a miracle baby at 1.5 pounds that wasn't supposed to live, then being diagnosed with a neurological disorder, Tourette's Syndrome (in the height of my TS growing up, jumping up and down, intense neck twitches, wrist flicking, multiple auditory noises, multiple facial expressions - and many times they would commingle), being the weird kid, dealing with adversity and bullying growing up - I wanted to give out the opposite of the negative I had received by others around me.

Don't get me wrong, I had a ton of positivity around me, but sometimes one negative can overshadow a river of positivity. Be a giver of good, positivity, love, light, strength and encouragement.

I know life is 10% what happens to me and 90% how I react to it. I know every breath I take is a gift. I know I have failed way more than I have succeeded in life and business, that I have learned from every step, and that I have gotten up every time, dusted myself off, and kept going, and that is why I have succeeded no matter the outcome. I know that I came to a platform like LinkedIn 18 years ago - with a purpose to give out good to the universe. I felt that no matter how bad my day was, no matter what happened to me, I would give out good 365 days a year with the hopes of achieving my "WHY."

To inspire one person a day.

If I can inspire one person to chase after their dreams (and know/feel/BELIEVE that they can accomplish ANYTHING). To get up one more time after they've failed 50,000 times, to believe in themselves that they CAN get back up and go again, and know that they ARE succeeding, EVERY time they do, regardless of achieving that goal. If I can inspire one person to inspire someone ELSE. If I can put a smile on one person's face for one brief moment during a time that they truly need it, or a laugh (which we all need now more than ever). Or I can make one person feel good about themselves when they just don't.

If I can do one of these things each day for one person, I have done my part as a human being to make the world a better place.

Life has, continues, and will continue to throw me mad curveballs. And I'll keep getting up to the plate and swinging. Because as my Mom said when I asked her, "Why did you put me in a lion's costume as my first costume as a baby (hand-made by Mom)?" "Because you're a fighter," she said. "You fought for every breath to make it into this world."

My hopes are that everyone will get up and fight. And keep getting up. And to believe in themselves and know that they have a voice, that they have a story, and that they matter. That their voice and story can and will positively impact and inspire another human being's life, and there is no greater gift to give and no greater gift to receive. To know, that they are not alone. And that especially in a world like Linkedin, we are all here to support one another. We are all in it together, we are better together, and we are stronger together.

My one last powerful word of inspiration I would like you all to take to heart and never forget from this day forward is "INSPIRE." I personally chose this word as you never know who you are inspiring by showing up, by being you and by sharing who you truly are.

"People may forget what you said, but they will never forget how you made them feel." - Maya Angelou

Brian Schulman

A 3X #1 Best-Selling Author and internationally known Keynote Speaker, Brian Schulman is known as the Godfather, and Pioneer, of LinkedIn Video and one of the world's premiere live streaming and video marketing experts who's insights have been featured on NASDAQ, ROKU and a #1 Best-selling live-streaming book.

With 20+ years of proven Digital Marketing experience strategizing with Fortune 500 brands across the globe, Brian founded and is the CEO of Voice Your Vibe, which brings his wealth of knowledge, as an advisor and mentor to Founders & C-Suite Executives by providing workshops and 1-on-1 Mastery Coaching on how to voice their vibe, attract their tribe, and tell a story that people will fall in love with through the power and impact of live and pre-recorded video.

Named "2020 Best LIVE Festive Show of The Year" at the IBM TV Awards, his global award-winning weekly LIVE shows #ShoutOutSaturday & #WhatsGoodWednesday have been featured in Forbes, Thrive Global, Yahoo Finance, an Amazon best-selling book and syndicated on a Smart TV Network. Among his many awards and honours, Brian has been named a 'LinkedIn Top Voice', 'LinkedIn Video Creator Of The Year,' one of the 'Top 50 Most Impactful People of LinkedIn' for three consecutive years and a 'LinkedIn Global Leader of The Year for two consecutive years. Beyond all the achievements and accolades, Brian is most proud of his two children and the connections and relationships he's made along the way.

Brian Schulman

Founder & CEO of Voice Your Vibe

858.692.7272 mobile

brian@voiceyourvibe.com

www.voiceyourvibe.com

linkedin.com/in/brianschulman

linkedin.com/company/voiceyourvibe

To be inspired is AMAZING. To inspire, is INCREDIBLE.

Watch and learn WHY: https://lnkd.in/geyi7WR

2021 Top 50 Most Impactful People Of LinkedIn

2021 3X #1 Best Selling Author, *The 13 Steps To Riches Volume 1, 2 & 3*

2020 Top 50 Most Impactful People Of LinkedIn

2020 Linkedin Global Leader Of the Year

2020 Best Festive LIVE Show of the Year at The IBM TV Awards

2019 LinkedIn Video Creator Of the Year

2019 Top 50 Most Influential Men Of LinkedIn

2019 Linkedin Global Leader Of the Year

2018 LinkedIn Top Voice

What We Are Here Learning Is What We Are Here To Teach

By Sally Anderson

There are A LOT of people hurting in the world right now with an unprecedented level of fear being experienced, so I wanted to provide some inspiration and motivation that *'This too shall pass.'* You will transition what you are experiencing…

When you come out of a storm you are not the same person that walked in – that's what the storm was all about – Haruki Murakami

Not all storms come to disrupt your life; some come to clear your path…

The devil whispered in my ear, 'You are not strong enough to weather the storm' – Today, I whispered in the devil's ear – I AM THE STORM!

I am a true believer that 'What we are here learning is what we are here to teach,' as referenced in the book *'Course Of Miracles'* by Drs. Helen Schucman and Bill Thetford. So my advice off the back of my own life apprenticeship, which I share below, is this: Look for the lessons, PERSPECTIVE is everything right now, and REMEMBER you are NEVER given anything that you cannot handle!

My unique life apprenticeship, traumatic history, and eventual mastery as a transformational leadership coach provide a rare combination of talents. Without a doubt, my life experiences laid the foundation for my vocation to partner with others to achieve a similar level of transcendence. My determination to regain my life from the most dehumanizing experience imaginable had me dedicate my life to partnering with others and shaped my personal development and destiny to become one of the most fearless leadership coaches on the planet.

Here are some of my learnings and subsequent teachings, which I share purely as a point of inspiration today:

- Inhumane cruelty to learn FORGIVENESS

- Extreme betrayal to learn EMPATHY

- Evil sadistic judgment to learn COMPASSION

- How to survive one of the worst reported gang rapes in the history of New Zealand by more than 100 mob members in the early 80's to learn what it means to DIE TO ONESELF

- What it means to go beyond the comprehension of human terror to teach what it means to LIVE AND LEAD A FEARLESS EXISTENCE

- What it means to live through 'hell on earth and achieve what quite literally is 'not survivable' to learn what it means to be 'SELF-ACTUALISED'

- Severe criticism, rejection to learn ACCEPTANCE

- Demonic inner critic to learn EQUANIMITY and PROFOUND PEACE

- Seething envy/jealousy to learn UNDERSTANDING

- Heinous bullying and ridicule to learn about BOUNDARIES AND SAFETY

- Targeted anger to learn HARMONY and JOY

- Physical and mental abuse beyond comprehension to learn TO COME HOME

- Psychological manipulation to learn WISDOM

- Abhorred persecution to learn SELF-LOVE, SELF-WORTH, SELF-VALUE

- Hatred and racial discrimination to learn UNCONDITIONAL LOVE

- Vengeful character assassination over nine months to learn ENLIGHTENMENT/TRANSCENDENCE

- Self-debilitating addictions to learn to SURRENDER

- Body dysmorphia to the extreme to learn to honour the body as THE VESSEL

- Sadness and constant disappointment to learn to TRUST

- Isolation, 'aloneness' and complete loss of control to learn about FAITH

- Psychotic mental mind gymnastics to learn how to MASTER the monkey mind

- Loss of any semblance of hope to learn what I am capable of SURVIVING

- Constant financial devastation to learn to allow SUPPORT and REINVENT

- Debilitating fear, anxiety and paranoia to learn the power of the BREATHE

- Narcissistic annihilation of a sadistic nature to learn ILLUMINATION to the next level

- To let go of masculine control to learn how to EMBRACE THE FEMININE and RECEIVE

- Sadistic self-sabotage to learn to LOVE MY INNER CHILD

Name an extremity of negative emotion, and I have transcended the experience

The reward from a life apprenticeship of this nature is the ability to facilitate real-time transformation for those who have disconnected from their soul essence. I consider it a profound privilege to stop people from hurting PERMANENTLY!

I get that the life apprenticeship that I have experienced is in perfection for what I am here to teach. So my question to you today from a perspective of motivation is this: What are you here learning that plays a part in what you are here to teach?

When the storm presents itself, I table this as an inquiry.

The series of questions I ask myself or dear friends in this sort of utterly surreal situation is always, "If I understand that this is happening not TO me, but FOR me, what is the blessing and opportunity here? What if the Universe has an exquisite plan for me, one that is so beautiful it would blind my eyes? What would that plan look like? How is this a beautiful 'divine redirection'? What have I been asked to surrender completely to? What scary move have I been ignoring or delaying that is now possible because I am at Tabula Rasa?"

You Are Never Given Anything You Cannot Handle!

Your Story Does Not Define Who You Are, BUT It Is The Backbone Of Your Character On How You Show Up In The World – Sally Anderson

This is a brave statement but one I live by. I frame the journey we are all on as human beings as one's 'life apprenticeship.' My only way of understanding why some people experience some things, and others do not is that we are all here learning different lessons. The life apprenticeship I have lived has been unique, complete with profound lessons that have served thousands of people to overcome their past and reclaim their power to live and lead fulfilling and rewarding lives sustainably.

I love bringing 'simplicity to complexity,' so I have focused on my top 12 recommendations for those that need this message today!

TOP 12 Recommendations

1. GET PRESENT TO THE COSTS – get that nothing will change until the costs of what you are experiencing outweigh the payoff of what you are getting out of staying in xyz state. Most people are disassociated from the costs, for if they were present to the costs, they would literally move in a heartbeat!

2. DO THE WORK – get the healing, get the coaching, and seek out SUPPORT! You are NEVER alone if you reach out and ask for support.

3. LEARN TO MEDITATE – get out of your head, get out of the monkey mind. ALL human suffering is a function of what we make things MEAN! The power of being at one with the breath devoid of the mind is priceless.

4. MORNING PRACTICES – get committed to putting petrol in the car (YOU) to go the distance (achieve your goals) at the speed you wish to go (urgency) to reach the destination (achieve your vision) – the no#1 success strategy of EVERY successful person on this planet is the application of morning practices, *i.e.,* fitness, food regime, gratitude, meditation, affirmations etc.

5. DO NOT COMPARE – get that your journey is your journey, no one has the right to judge YOUR journey, honour your unique life apprenticeship and STOP comparing yourself to others.

6. DO NOT PSYCHOANALYSE – get how ludicrous it is to stay in the vicious cycle of asking WHY xyz occurred; you can do nothing about the past (it is what it is), BUT you can do something about the future. STOP the analysis/paralysis battle and realize that if you have been dealt the cards, you have what it takes to deal with it.

7. LEARN EXPERIENTIAL FORGIVENESS – get that the focus of your forgiveness needs to be less on the event, happening, or perpetrator/s and more on yourself for what you have done to yourself. Most hang out in analytical forgiveness v experiential

forgiveness – how do you know the difference? If you have truly forgiven experientially, your past is no longer in your future.

8. YOU CREATE YOUR REALITY – get that you are the creator of your reality, and if your reality is not what you want it to be, you are the only one that can change that! How many books do we need to read that state, 'Be careful what you think — your thoughts create your reality?' Well, they do! Be extra vigilant with where your thoughts are focused on a moment-by-moment, day-by-day basis and watch your world transform.

9. FAITH and LOVE ARE EVERYTHING – get that you were born fearless, born connected and born intuitive. This was your birthright; then, you learned at an early age to separate from this innate state. To reconnect is a function of trusting the unknown again, embracing uncertainty again, learning to love again, and realizing that all the magic lies in coming home to your higher power. LOVE is all there is. Faith (whatever that is for you) is about trusting the unknown as much as the known – what you could accomplish in your life if you trust the unknown as much as the known is unfathomable!

10. THE POWER OF CHOICE – get that you have a CHOICE on how you feel, CHOICE on how you react/respond, CHOICE on what you do, CHOICE on how you do it, CHOICE on what your life looks like from this day forward. We are ALWAYS at the CHOICE moment by moment. The choices that you make every moment of every day will be the measurement of your level of commitment in your life.

11. COMMITMENT = RESULTS – get that wherever the results are being produced in your life is a barometer on your current level of commitment – that can land like a 'cup of cold sick' for some. A high percentage of people believe that they are committed but are not experiencing the results that they want in their life. I am here today to inform you that if your life is not where you want it to be, a

high percentage of the reason will lie squarely in your relationship with 'what it means to truly be committed."

12. ACKNOWLEDGE – get that you cannot transform that which you cannot own. If you cannot own that you are irresponsible, a victim, a martyr, a saboteur, etc., you cannot transform it. Acknowledging the reality of a situation is the breakthrough (without default-based meaning), and from this space, you can then determine how you wish to transition from this experience or not; you are at choice!

Just remember, you are never given ANYTHING you cannot handle – STOP fighting 'what is' and know I speak from profound experience to make this statement. I have traversed some of the most dehumanizing experiences a human being can comprehend. I have dedicated my life to teaching others how to navigate the terrain from victim to victor and, more importantly, knowing how to sustain this state. Honour YOUR unique life apprenticeship to this point. For those that need to hear this message today know it is meant to be.

Traditional Leadership Is Dead

I have spent the last three decades specializing in the leadership space globally. I am passionate about contributing to the evolution of consciousness for those who lead. I died on the block at age 15 and was resurrected of my own accord; I am very clear I should not be here today, but I am. I believe my entire purpose for being is to give back what I have learned.

Covid 19 has highlighted the massive level of fear evident in our society globally. As much as there is a viral pandemic at play, there is also a fear pandemic at play. To be fearful means that you distrust the unknown realm, you do not embrace uncertainty and have not integrated all facets of your existence psychologically.

As a generalization, we as a society are somewhat disconnected and disassociated due to a lack of education on how to evolve one's consciousness beyond the known realm. We still teach the same things in our education system globally; we still teach standard linear education at the leadership level. Leaders, I believe, yawn at the prospect of yet another leadership retreat, leadership development training, for they are already unconsciously competent in the linear left-brain skills of traditional leadership. The standard response from a number of CEOs I have received in the past specifically is this: Can you just come in and fix my people???? In these instances, at no point would they consider that they themselves need to look at how they operate!

I believe acts of God, like tornadoes, tsunamis, bushfires, floods, earthquakes, pandemics and the like, are awakening the consciousness of the planet en mass – if we are not willing to listen, then the universe, in its wisdom, will make us listen. There is nothing like raising awareness and raising consciousness when you are forced to. Here's the irony, the social distancing/lockdown and separation are creating connections unlike we have ever witnessed.

Could we return to what we perceived as normal pre-Covid? The newly coined phrase of the 'new normal' post-Covid-19 is an interesting prospect. What does that look like? Do we welcome it? Are we ready for the transition? For this to occur, we cannot do this by operating from the same paradigm we did before! Traditional leadership, in my opinion, is dead due to the limitation of its teachings. You cannot access the limitless potential of the unknown realm unless you let go of the known realm. Leaders who were unwilling to evolve, change, and grow before are now being forced to. To transition powerfully as a human race, we need to embrace a new frontier in leadership development. So what do I recommend?

Top 10 Recommendations:

1. If you are the head of the organization, then facilitate a conversation with yourself and your executive team on what the new normal could look like. Do you embrace change? Do you embrace uncertainty? Do you have practices in place as a team to deal with fear individually and collectively in a way that excites you rather than operate as an unspoken undercurrent?

2. What is the current status of your leadership development strategy and professional development strategy for your leaders and your people? Will it address what is required in the new normal? If not, what are you doing about it?

3. Do you have a culture that embraces personal and professional development – do you utilize external and or internal coaches within your culture? Are you ready for the change that is at hand? Do you know how to transition? Will you elicit the right support?

4. If you are the head of the organization, have you arrived at the juncture of realization that you cannot operate as you did before? Have you asked yourself this question? What are your blindspots, and are you actively going to work on these?

5. Do you know the current climate of your culture? Have you interviewed everyone in the organization to understand the state of those managing your organization? Have you elicited their feedback, and do you welcome their feedback? Do you have an integral understanding of what your people are experiencing? What are you doing to support them in their transition?

6. Have you moved from surviving this experience to getting excited about the potential of this experience? If not, what are you doing to make this transition as powerful as possible? And are you willing to elicit the right support to make this happen?

7. Future pacing yourself and your organization could be a powerful process. Could you introduce different working hours, more flexibility around working location, some from the office, some from home, or a mix of both, customized for each individual? Flexibility around incentive schemes, allowing people to start later to care for their children and work later? Are you encouraging time at the gym during the day, paying for gym memberships under incentive? The list is endless of what you could co-create together – it's an opportunity to listen to your people and assess what they want – the happier they are, the bigger the benefit to the culture and organization.

8. Have you put a stop to off-the-shelf type traditional leadership and staff training? This type of training historically is a waste of money due to the very questionable ROI back to the business.

9. Have you considered training where there is 'skin in the game' by your people? Telling people to go on a training course and paying for them is just crazy. This does not serve the individual and does not serve the organization. Unless there is 'skin in the game,' they will not take responsibility to apply what they have learned – knowledge, unless applied, is completely redundant!

10. Uncomfortability, resistance and confrontation are the cornerstones to true transformation – unless you yourself and your organization have changed your relationship with these three emotions, you will never achieve the transformation you seek! FACT. So, to what degree do you, as a leader or your organization, go looking to be confronted, go looking to be resistant, go looking to be uncomfortable, knowing that unless you do, you will stay in the current paradigm of the limited known realm? There are always two contexts to everything, the empowered context and the disempowered context. The context about which I speak here is the empowered context of confrontation, resistance and

uncomfortability! As change agents, it is our responsibility to keep pushing the boundaries on what we know.

Going back to what we perceived as normal is sheer ludicracy! You need to prepare, you need to rise above the inertia of day-to-day busyness, fear and survival and take charge of your new direction! AND GET EXCITED. This is the most powerful time in history to co-create, and co-design the new future!

Have You Ever Achieved Anything in Your Life That You Never Thought You Could Achieve?

I would like to remind you that it is rare not to find a person who hasn't already achieved something in their life that they never thought they could achieve – if you have found evidence in one domain of your life, then it is possible in any other domain.

To demonstrate, I thought I would share ten areas of my life where I achieved something I never thought I could but then did. Who I was in the old identity and who I am in the new identity is like night and day. This fuels me to know; it's a knowing, which is far more powerful than a belief, that if I can achieve what I have to date, then there is nothing that I cannot achieve as I traverse and navigate my life apprenticeship from this point forward. I share these as a point of inspiration today.

I am in awe of the power of the human spirit. I have listened to thousands of awe-inspiring stories over the last three decades as a leadership coach, and it never ceases to amaze me what people are capable of accomplishing if they master their mindset!

1. Decades of extreme body dysmorphia to competing in body sculpting, coming 2nd in my first competition, 56kg, 8% body fat – hundreds of hours of posing training, hundreds of hours of mirror work in 6-inch high heel shoes/hundreds of hours of choreography training/hundreds of hours of weight training/hundreds of hours of

cardio / highly disciplined food regime – maintained that lifestyle for three years post-competing

2. My biggest fear was public speaking; I was terrified of people to commanding a global professional keynote speaking career spanning 2+ decades

3. Lived into two decades of belief that I was dumb and could not write to being a published author of 2 books, the 2nd which I wrote in 90 days. Daily I am recognized and acknowledged for my writing ability due to the extent to which I generate value add content on a weekly basis

4. Never thought I would ever find love; who would want a woman like me, so damaged and so soiled to now being married for 11 years to the most extraordinary man

5. Never thought I could run my own business to now having been in private practice for over 19+ years internationally coaching at the highest level of leadership

6. Always wanted to work in New York City, but it was only ever a dream to leading a global restructure program of 3000 projects in The Netherlands/Boston and NEW YORK – our offices were five blocks from ground zero

7. Had THE worst inner critic on the planet 24/7 high volume, could never turn it off to now mastering the realm of equanimity for over a decade and 3+ decades of disciplined meditation practice - worked with Shaolin Monks/Qi gong masters

8. Due to my belief that I was dumb and could not write, I never thought I could develop my own intellectual property and yet have created my own co-creative leadership curriculum that has touched on and changed thousands of lives globally

9. Never thought that I could coach and make a difference in someone else's life to having trained as a master coach with over 100

coaches in my methodology and now coach at the highest level of leadership, *i.e.*, CEOs, C-Suite, Leading Influencers, Celebrities, Politicians, Millionaires and Billionaires. 19 years in private practice and thousands of lives transformed

10. Always wanted to lead my own retreats but never thought I could to developing my own 3-day leadership curriculum and leading these retreats throughout the globe for ten months of the year for ten years, transforming thousands of people's lives

So I ask you today, 'What Have You Ever Achieved in YOUR LIFE That You Never Thought You Could Achieve BUT then did? I am here to tell you today that through the power of belief; you can ACHIEVE ANYTHING!!!!!! MAYBE there is no coincidence that you are reading this today!

Your story does not define who you are, but your story is the backbone of your character for how you show up in the world – Sally Anderson

One word of inspiration I would like to leave you with is **Equanimity**. Equanimity is the highest state of consciousness to achieve in this lifetime to sustain living and leading in an empowered state regardless of circumstance; it goes beyond 'self-actualization'- you cannot put a dollar value on living in an equanimous state

"If there are more stars in the galaxy than there are grains of salt on every beach, desert of this planet of ours, it is beyond our comprehension what we can tap into." – Sally Anderson

Sally Anderson

Sally is at the forefront of 'sustainable' human and organizational transformation.

She has developed a leadership curriculum which is a global first, specializing in sustainable transformation personally ans professionally.

Sally has privately coached key influencers internationally: CEOs/C-Suiteexecutives/teams/entrepreneurs/celebrities /politicians /millionaires/billionaires for over 20 years.

Linkedin-linkedin.com/in/sallyanderson-leadershipcoachtothein fluencers/

Email: Sally@sallyandersoninternational.com

A Journey of Profound Lessons Through Time

By Brian J. Esposito

My story started at the very young age of 8 years old when I truly learned the value of hard work and what it felt like to create something. I was always eager to go to my father's warehouse and manufacturing facility, where they developed fingernail care treatment products. I will always remember how exciting it was and the great sense of pride I felt when I would physically fill, assemble, and package a bottle of FingerMates' Formula 10 Original Nail Hardener for a customer. From that moment, I was bit by the entrepreneur bug. I also feel that for certain people, it's just in one's blood and DNA. Since then, I have always wanted to feel that amazing sense not only of accomplishment but also that wonderful feeling of working with a team and providing opportunities for people to earn and make a good living. Unfortunately, the journey I have been on has been constantly balanced with great moments met with awful situations. However, I wouldn't trade the experiences for anything.

One specific situation that happened to me was in February of 2016 when a drunk driver hit me head-on in a car collision. My entire world collapsed from dealing with health and well-being issues and quickly realizing that I was surrounded by the wrong people who were not competent in their roles, nor was their dedication to me or the company in the right place. I lost everything, I had to rebuild with less than nothing, and I had to do it from a mental state of not being bitter, jaded, or angry. I became grateful that this woman hit me, as I am still here, and she could have killed someone, and that accident forced me to change my entire work and business model, as my model was horribly wrong prior. I am proud of the man that I have become, and I found strengths that I never knew I had or ever knew I needed.

The harder the journey, the more rewarding the outcome. One of the important parts of growth and evolving is that no matter how dark it gets, and for me, I did see the devil, is that one does not lose themselves in the process. Learning, becoming smarter, and wiser does not have to mean that you become jaded or bitter. That's the hardest part, as it's quite easy to be angry and hate the world, especially when one is feeling attacked from all sides and you do not know whom to trust or confide in. I've learned that there is always a solution and that one must find a way to filter through everyone one comes in contact with and to build and maintain a small, positive, supportive inner circle.

It was not easy to get past this and overcome my past, especially during certain specific situations; however, I knew I could not succeed, grow, and pick myself up when I was kicked to the ground if I had to also battle internal demons. That meant no matter how hard it got; I could not cry, "why me," or be mad or upset with the people that put me in the situation I was in because the reality is that it was my fault and doing that allowed me to be in that situation. The most successful thing to date for me was to stop giving other people my mindset and wondering why people do certain things or say certain things. They were not raised in my household, nor went through my exact life experiences. It would not be rational for me to believe that anyone would think, act, react, operate, maneuver, or respond exactly how I would in life. Having that peace of mind allowed me not to waste time wondering about things that were out of my control and also allowed me to focus on my own personal growth, the real business opportunities I could create, and how to properly value myself going forward.

Lessons Learned in Difficult Times are Priceless

First and foremost, it's imperative to know that in life you are not being picked on. Everyone goes through problems, and more success, or money, does not mean fewer problems. That equals the playing field and allows you to know that you are not alone.

Next, always remember that time is your most precious commodity. Know when, where, on what, and with whom to share that precious time with, and experience as many "bad" people as you possibly can as early as you can. You will have a lot more to lose later in life when you are more established if you are not well-seasoned or have experienced all of life's wonderful characters and actors. As you grow and evolve, and the more pain you have been through, the more prepared you are to handle any situation and become a well-rounded entrepreneur, founder, or senior-level executive.

In addition to the above, always remember to ask for help and eliminate from your mind that asking for assistance is weak. Drop your pride and show vulnerabilities. There are wonderful people in this world that are available and willing to help. You will never know who they are or where they are if you don't open the door for them to see the real you.

The one word of inspiration I would like to leave you with today is Consistency. Being consistent in your actions is so important to your personal brand and what people expect out of you. There is a caveat to this, however. You need to be consistent from a place of good ethical values and morals. Being consistently a "jerk" will get you nowhere in life.

Also, be consistent in your personal life decisions and actions as well as your professional ones. Be someone that not only others can count on but someone that you can also count on as well.

Consistent actions will result in consistent healthy results. If your actions are resulting in poor returns, then you need to analyze what you are doing wrong, what needs to change and work on it slowly and correctly.

Life is a long race; you do not have to finish first; you just need to finish and accomplish the goals and dreams you set out to do, what makes you happy, and what your life's purpose is.

"Everyone can be an overnight success if you were to wake up each new day a little smarter, a little wiser, and a little stronger than the day before." - Brian J. Esposi

Brian Esposito

Ranked among the world's Top 10 CEOs for 2020 in The World CEO Rankings Awards by Adria Management, LLC, Brian J. Esposito is the founder and CEO of Esposito Intellectual Enterprises, LLC (EIE). An award-winning serial entrepreneur and business leader, recently renowned for being a core part of an innovative team to build *Nodle* — the world's largest wireless network and ecosystem of connected devices, as well as the creator of the *Nodle Cash App*, where anyone around the world can passively earn cryptocurrency. In addition, also being a core part of team *TurnCoin* and the launch of *VirtualStax* through TheXchange. TheXchange is the company behind *VirtualStaX* and the *VirtualStaX App*: A people-driven platform that empowers individuals to achieve their dreams while giving their fans a vehicle to support them, share in their journey, and participate in their success. TheXchange currently has the public support of Drew Brews, Patrick Mahomes, Randy Jackson, and Jean de Villiers — and for one of his early businesses, which ranked among The Fastest-Growing Private Companies by Inc. 5000 for six consecutive years.

In December 2019, Brian was featured in *The Corporate Investment Times*, the next-gen investment magazine in the Middle

East. With over 20 years of experience in high-profile executive roles involving complex business challenges and high-stakes decisions, he founded *Esposito Intellectual Enterprises (EIE)*. Wholly owned by himself, EIE currently consists of 75+ entities, 150+ joint ventures that have been accumulated around the world that are participating in 25+ industry focuses, or just one degree separating any industry or market that Brian may want to enter into and do business in. With a technique that he spent years perfecting, he connects not only the right people but the right people at the right time.

"Integrity is at the core of who we are and what we do at EIE. We strive to do good business with good people,"

Brian J. Esposito

CEO and Founder

Esposito Intellectual Enterprises, LLC

website: www.eie.rocks

email: brian@eie.rocks

Twitter: @brianjesposito

LinkedIn: https://www.linkedin.com/in/brianjesposito/

A Choice to Surrender

By Emily Rodger

Growing up, the opportunity to participate in sports was not readily available to me. My parents separated when I was five years old, and most of my life was spent with my mom and three sisters (I'm the second youngest).

When I graduated from high school, I just wanted to become someone — I wanted to make something of my life. I became a dental hygienist, bought my first house, and started travelling the world. I was so curious about life and the world and all it had to offer.

At 27, a friend of mine gifted me a road bike. I was very involved with fitness at the time — teaching fitness classes and staying very active — but competitive sport was something I didn't have much experience with. When I got on this bike, though, I felt strong, capable and, for the first time in my life, confident.

I competed in my first-ever bike race in 2013 (finishing among the top riders). A few days later, I was out for a ride when a driver ran a stop sign and hit me.

I will never forget realizing the driver was not going to stop. At that moment, I knew I would be hit. I knew both me and the car were going fast enough for me to be seriously injured.

My life flashed before my eyes in the fraction of the second I had to react. I remember letting go of my bike's handlebars and telling myself to relax my body before I received the full impact of this SUV. I flew through the air, landing head-first and then hitting the left side of my face on the pavement.

I immediately went unconscious.

During the time I was lying on the road unconscious, I had an out-of-body experience and somehow knew what had just happened to me. I felt at peace and wasn't scared — I was with God. I remember hearing God say to me, Emily, this is not your time [to pass on]. I briefly regained consciousness to find myself lying face-first in a pool of my own blood. I couldn't move or feel my body. I knew my face was seriously injured, and I could hear my then-boyfriend, who I was on the ride with, screaming my name, thinking I was dead.

The trauma I experienced during that accident haunted me for years, yet I did everything I could to try to avoid facing what I had gone through. I returned to racing six months after the accident. All I wanted to do was forget everything that had happened to me. I wanted all my (visible) injuries to be erased, so I underwent countless scar reduction treatments on my face just to get rid of any sign that I had been hurt. I thought these treatments would take away the emotional trauma I was experiencing, and I just wanted people to stop asking how I was doing.

In the year following the accident, I raced 21 races, podiumed 17, and won 14. All that mattered was people seeing me as someone who was strong — who survived what could have been a life-threatening accident and came out a champion. I used the bike as a tool to help me avoid all that I was feeling. I lived in constant fear of getting hurt again, and there were many times when I was afraid to fall asleep because of the nightmares I would inevitably have. When I did manage to sleep, I was afraid I wouldn't wake up.

I was battling a brain injury — I didn't even recognize myself anymore. Triggered by seemingly everything, I experienced personality changes and would be easily angered. I hated who I had become; I just wanted the "old me" back.

I couldn't think straight.

I was anxious all the time.

I had to write notes for everything just so I could remember what I was supposed to do next.

I just wanted to be by myself so no one could see how much I was struggling.

I felt so alone in that season. Nobody really knew what I was going through, and I wanted it that way, but I was so scared of what was happening to me and terrified that I would never return to "normal." There were so many aspects of my recovery/injuries, thoughts, and feelings that I felt like I didn't have control over, and I hated not having control. The bike gave me a sense of control — I could control how much I trained, how hard I trained, and (for the most part) the outcome of races. The bike became a distraction for me; it gave me a purpose at a time when I was struggling to find any purpose in life.

I never dreamt of being an elite athlete when I was a kid; it wasn't something I even thought was possible, let alone achievable. But here I was, a few years after my accident and racing at the professional level. I became a 2x UCI GranFondo World Champion (both Time Trial and Road Race), Canadian Masters National Time Trial Champion, and 70.3 Ironman world qualifier. I loved the lifestyle I was living — I was a full-time athlete, and my focus was on training. I never loved the competitive side of the sport, many people probably thought that's what I truly enjoyed about racing, but it wasn't — I loved to train, I loved to be alone and push myself to the absolute max when nobody was watching.

By 2017 I started being more honest with myself by exploring the choices I was making and the path I was on. I knew I had to make some changes, really difficult ones. I had worked so hard to get to where I was in cycling, but at what expense?

It was nearing the end of that summer, and my final races of the season were going to be held in France. I made the commitment to myself that once I returned from racing overseas, I would spend the next couple of months with family and friends and stop making everything about me and the bike.

I went to France to race UCI GranFondo World Championships and then compete at what would have been my final race of the season. The night before Worlds, my dad called to tell me my grandma had passed away. It hurt to know that I was so far from home when she died. I thought about all the times I had chosen the bike over being with family and how many times I was not physically present with them. I had a lot of guilt.

I got up the next morning and rolled to the starting line of the race with tears in my eyes as I questioned the choices I was making. But as the race started, I went back to the headspace I loved to be in … just me and the bike (and hundreds of competitive, eager-to-win riders beside me). I had one goal, and that was to win. I had trained for this race for months, visualized every climb, descent, every possible move, and I could see the race unfolding before me moment by moment. Never once in that race did I doubt my ability—I was strong, capable, worthy, and I believed in myself the entire time.

I raced fearlessly. I pushed myself past every breaking point, I dug deeper than I ever had before, and I crossed the finish line with my arms up in the air, soaking in the cheers of the crowd as I relished in the moment of winning my second World Champion title. I loved the thrill of winning, of feeling like I was finally good enough, that I had finally done something with my life. But it also made me sad to think that I needed a bike race to make me feel that way about myself, and deep down, I really just wanted to be home. It was the first time in my cycling career, after years spent on the road, that I was homesick.

I debated flying home to be with my family after that race, but I had made a commitment with a team to race the following week, so I chose my commitment to the team. Looking back, I always had a bad feeling about that final stage race, there were plenty of red flags telling me I should never have raced in it, but my ego and pride got the best of me.

Three-fourths of the way through the first stage of the race, I was descending a mountain and came around a sharp left-hand turn to see a vehicle approaching me on a narrow, single-lane road. There was a rock wall to my left, a deep ditch, and then a cliff to my right.

The thing I had feared the absolute most in life was about to happen again.

I slammed on my brakes as hard as I could, and I went flying through the air. I put my arms out to stop myself as I came crashing down on the pavement. Adrenaline quickly took over as I stood up, knowing that I had broken bones, but I still stumbled to grab my bike so I could finish the race.

I could barely stand, I couldn't see straight, I was in the most excruciating pain I had ever been in, and yet I just wanted my bike. I stumbled off to the side of the road and went unconscious. I woke up numerous times. I could hear someone standing on the road, and I kept screaming for him to call for help — I couldn't understand why an ambulance wasn't already there for me, and I didn't know why no one was directly with me to assist.

The fear of sustaining another brain injury and falling asleep, only to not wake up, was all I could think about as I drifted in and out of consciousness. I lay in that ditch for an hour and 30 minutes before an ambulance finally picked me up and drove me to a hospital that was over two hours away.

I spent eight days in the hospital until I could fly back to Canada. Those long days and nights brought back so many memories of my time alone in the hospital after my first accident. I was in complete disbelief that I had been hit again, that the thing I feared the most had happened a second time.

But no matter how alone I was, I always felt the presence of God and knew I was taken care of.

While I was in that hospital, I thought a lot about fly fishing. I would try to imagine myself on the water as a way to cope with the physical pain I was experiencing. I began fly fishing a couple of years after my first accident. I was still living in Arizona at the time and would go up to Oak Creek in Sedona on my recovery days from training. I loved just sitting by the water, away from everything and everyone. During those moments of stillness, I wasn't thinking about my injuries, my accident, racing, or all the fear and anxiety I was living with — I was simply captivated by trying to spot trout. It was during those days spent fishing that my memories of fishing as a child came back to me. I remembered being four or five years old and trying to catch trout in a brook by my childhood home. I remembered so vividly the joy I experienced when I was finally able to catch even one.

As I lay in the hospital bed, I visualized the water flowing downstream. Those thoughts reminded me that these hard times would pass, but I was going to need to swim upstream to get back to where I wanted to go. I thought about Atlantic salmon and the challenges they face while returning to their natal rivers — their journey is far from easy. From the river to the ocean, then back to the river, these fish constantly face challenges. They fight their way through countless predators, push through fishing nets, endure environmental changes, and relentlessly leap up waterfalls, often just to get knocked down over and over again. They also know when to be patient — sitting in pools when water levels drop or temperatures get too high — timing is everything. I've learned that patience and perseverance go hand-in-hand. There are times when we need to work hard, push through, and persevere, but there are also times when we just need to be still, rest and be patient. I needed rest; I needed to be patient. These salmon are ultimately just trying to return home, and that is all I wanted … to be home.

People often ask me where I get my strength — my strength to push through no matter how many times I get knocked down — physically, emotionally, and mentally. Simply put, my strength comes from God.

I've always had a personal relationship with Christ ever since I was a young girl, but this relationship strengthened during my accidents. God was the one who was always there for me — He saved my life, He has given me second, third, fourth, hundreds of chances, and He has always been patient with me. He has caught me in mid-air to soften my fall, picked me up when I have been knocked down, and revealed Himself to me time and time again. I would not be where I am today if it were not for my faith. I can do all things through He who gives me strength (Philippians 4:13). I am reminded of this on a daily basis.

Cycling opened my eyes to a world I didn't even know existed, but stepping back from the sport I loved opened my eyes to an even greater world.

There have been many moments where I wished I could race or ride as fearlessly as I did before my second accident. There are times when I can get on my bike and let those fears go, but there are also many times when I remember just how dangerous the sport can be. There was a point in my life where the rewards far outweighed the risks, but that is no longer the case for me.

I have gone through countless surgeries, years of recovery and rehabilitation. I went from working as a dental hygienist to being the one in the dental chair receiving all the treatment.

This past year I was getting ready to begin filming a documentary on my story when I found out the bone around my front tooth had resorbed, and I would need to have that tooth extracted and receive a new bone graft, dental implant, etc. I feared that my tooth would fall out during filming, and for the first time in years, I had a moment where I was incredibly angry at the woman who had run the stop sign in Arizona and t-boned me. That accident was eight years ago, and here I was, still going through treatment. I managed to complete filming without losing my tooth and then had dental surgery after we finished the documentary. I woke up from surgery to find out that the bone loss had been more extensive than the dentist had thought. My dentist was not able to confidently place an immediate implant. As I lay in the dental chair, missing my front tooth, it brought me back to being in the hospital after my first accident and missing my teeth. I knew how long that road to recovery had been, and here I was, about to embark on it again. I felt defeated. Time and time again in my life, I have felt so defeated.

I burst into tears when I looked at myself in the mirror — it was the loudest, hardest cry I had let out in a very long time. Why did I have to keep going through this? When was I just going to be able to hop on the easy road in life?! I allowed myself to feel all those feelings, and then I made a choice — the choice to learn from this situation, the choice to be gentle with myself, to love myself unconditionally, and to show the world who I was, no matter what I looked like. Missing a front tooth does not define me, same as being an athlete did not define me. I am the same person — I am Emily — and by choosing to show up fully as Emily, I can give people the greatest gift of all: the space for them to fully show up as themselves.

For years I hid my struggles. All I cared about was people seeing me as someone who was strong. My definition of strength has expanded — strength does not only show up as being an elite athlete; strength is when we continually embrace who we are and rise back up, no matter how many times we get knocked down. I am grateful that I wasn't given an easy path in life; I am grateful for my hardships and the lessons I was able to learn along the way because they have shaped me into the woman I am today.

We will all face challenges in this life — many we don't see coming — but it's up to each of us to make a choice when those challenges do come. We can either sit in our grief and feel sorry for ourselves, like I was tempted to do after my accidents, or we can rely on God and that strength and courage we each have inside of us to become an even better, stronger, and truer version of ourselves. I, for one, am choosing the latter option. Which will you choose?

The one inspirational word I would like to leave you with today is "Surrender." To let go of my own worldly desires in life — the ones based on fear and the need to control. I choose (even when it's difficult at times) to remain humble and lean on God to show me the way, to surrender my will in order to receive His perfect will for my life.

"Our deepest fear is not that we are inadequate. Our deepest fear is that we are powerful beyond measure. It is our light, not our darkness, that most frightens us. We ask ourselves, 'Who am I to be brilliant, gorgeous, talented, fabulous?' Actually, who are you not to be? You are a child of God. Your playing small does not serve the world. There is nothing enlightened about shrinking so that other people won't feel insecure around you. We are all meant to shine, as children do. We were born to make manifest the glory of God that is within us. It's not just in some of us; it's in everyone. And as we let our own light shine, we unconsciously give other people permission to do the same. As we are liberated from our own fear, our presence automatically liberates others."

— Marianne Williamson, *A Return to Love: Reflections on the Principles of "A Course in Miracles"*

Emily Rodger

Emily Rodger is a Certified Executive and Leadership Coach, public speaker, author, former elite cyclist, and avid outdoorswoman. Her story is currently being featured in two documentaries: *Cadence: Breaking Rhythm and Finding Pace*—available through film festivals worldwide—and *Chasing The Current*, a one-hour documentary available on CBC television.

www.emilysrodger.com

LinkedIn: www.linkedin.com/in/emily-s-rodger

HOPE IS A BLIND TRUST IN ACTION

Hope is a supernatural gift of God by which we confidently wait for the evidence of things revealed!

By Amb. Chukwuemeka Innocent Amadi

HOPE is the point attained in our spiritual living by which we wait to validate God's mercy of revelation. It's always a preparatory step towards validation of one's faith in God's words, decrees, doctrines and commandments. When we hope for the validation of God's mercy of revelation in us; what we are simply doing is surrendering to God all our thoughts, ways, intelligence and know-how.

Hope is a blind trust in the proficiency and efficacy of God's word. This may be either demonstrated through our testimony, works of charity, praises offered selflessly to God, confessions in righteousness, deliberate avoidance of temptation, and not falling to sin.

Hope in God cannot be overestimated on the achieving front. Abraham hoped upon God! It was Abraham's Hope that graduated into Faith, and as such, Abraham was qualified to be righteous because his Hope built up to the level of faith, and God was pleased with him.

We must exercise Hope always act as conduits of HOPE. "Timothe, keep" what you Receive, pass it on to others. If we have received the grace of Hope, we must not kill it by our disbelief or doubt but rather nurture our hope and equally let it be infectious, spreading from us to others around us.

As believers in God's way our confident hope is that our God is alive to all our needs and responsibilities. This is true for every believer of God's word. We are hopeful of receiving a crown of righteousness like the apostle Paul mentioned in the scriptures.

What keeps us alive is our hope! This is not necessarily faith but "Hope."

When we lose hope, we automatically surrender our victory and our testimony to the devil! It's our stored hope that matures into our faith to obtain or access God's promises. We need to protect our hope jealously, and by that, I mean we need to continue to hope and not faint!

I would like to share my story of Hoping in God for his mercy. I had a peculiar situation after graduating with my first degree: I had obtained a Bachelor degree in Textile Science and Technology at the Ahmadu Bello University Zaria, Nigeria. Although it was a 5-year course, I had spent about eight years in school. Amidst the Civil disobedience/Workers strike actions between 2001-2004 in major Nigerian Universities, there were no admissions for the year 2003 as a result. During this time, we were meant to go back home to our parents, and I was living in the university area as my parents are both academic and administrative staff there.

The long wait for the civil action to be called off had come with a lot of challenges, and our hope of graduating on time was seriously put to the test. At the appointed time, God spoke, and today it's all a memory. I also faced a lot of challenges after graduation. I was hoping to receive my mandatory call-up letter to participate in the National Youth Service Corp (NYSC) scheme, which entails that every fresh graduate from the Nigeria University dedicates one (1) full year to serve our nation by being deployed to a different state from our place of birth or state of origin. I waited for four years to be deployed. Each year three badges of deployment are made, and cumulatively I had missed out on 12 possible deployment badges/terms. The issue with this is that you can't be meaningfully employed by the government without a NYSC discharge certificate, and you may not be able to progress with your Masters's degree without submitting a discharge certificate. I was stuck, challenged mentally and physically as well. I had prayed, made all the necessary follow up and even complained to the authorities, including making visits to the Academic Secretary's Office together with the Head of my Department, and it was all in vain. I received a lot of revelation concerning the issue, that I had to pray, fast and take up some spiritual exercises to keep my hope alive. At the appointed time, God intervened. I called a friend of mine who followed me to the office of the academic secretary, and we approached the administrators handling student files at that time. Initially, they refused to honour the request by the Academic Secretary to search for my file, but on that fateful day, I got a revelation from God to make a visit to the office and that things would be sorted out. That day my friend and I approached the administrator. Seeing that my friend was from another faith and not a Christian, he dressed in religious attire, and when we spoke to the man, he said it was an archived case and files of that type are really difficult to process. After a little persuasion, he asked that we return at noon to see if he had located my file.

The file in question took four hours to locate, and when we arrived at his office just before the time he gave us, there was my file lying on his desk. He asked me if I could confirm that it was my file, and I said, "Yes, sir!" My file was processed, and I was deployed for the NYSC scheme.

The much-awaited hope of resolution and deployment was lasting and came with a lot of faith as well. I had to remain resolute and strong in my Hope that I would one day be deployed for the NYSC scheme; I did, and today it's history.

God has a plan for each one of us, and God's plans prompt our hope to be alive and waiting. Hope keeps things fresh and vibrant in our spiritual lives.

Romans Chapter 5 verses 3-5

3. We can rejoice too, when we run into problems and trials, for we know that they help us develop endurance.

4. And endurance develops strength of character, and character strengthens our confident HOPE of salvation.

5. And this HOPE will not lead to disappointment. For we know how dearly God loves us because he has given us the Holy Spirit to fill our hearts with his love.

If we can make it through the darkest night, there is a brighter day coming!

Isaiah 60:19

"No longer will the sun be your light by day Or the moon be your light by night; I, the Lord, will be your eternal light; The light of my glory will shine on you.

I have chosen these inspirational scriptures from ISAIAH 60 because it reminds my subconscious mind that my source of hope is from the Lord and not from what is seen or felt by man.

I received a revelation from God in September 2009, when I had a divine encounter with God during my journey of conversion from worldliness to grace as a believer!

I was at a prayer meeting when other brethren didn't turn up, and I decided to pray on my own in the church.

While I was deep in prayer and praise to our Father Yahweh Elohim, the word of God came to me and said:

"Go to the book of Isaiah 60 and read; that's my promise to you if you will serve me!"

Although I had never taken note of that chapter before, I quickly took my bible and read it. It was amazing, and ever since, I have believed God's promises to me from his holy scripture in Isaiah 60. Furthermore, God led me to Isaiah 49 — this equally confirms God's promises to me.

I have been a living testimony to these words from God in my life for many years now, and it's still true in my life. Hallelujah.

Amb. Chukwuemeka Innocent Amadi

Amb. Chukwuemeka Innocent Amadi is a Peace Advocate and Sports Diplomat, Philanthropist, Environmentalist and the founder of *American Football For African Mission - AFFAM*; a Nonprofit NGO which uses football as a vehicle to reach out to the children and Youth of Africa, offering them hope, mentorship as well as a career pathway towards actualizing their God-given potential and attaining excellence through our Football Purposeful-play, Educational Curriculum; Charity and Peace Advocacy initiatives. Chukwuemeka is a World Peace Ambassador with the World Peace Tracts; a pioneer of Football development in Africa- who have created a dozen or more football teams, Youth League; the Africa Region Scouting Advisor to the ALL22 Global Scouting Network; signed up MOUs with six Football Federations across Africa; helped to offer hope to elite football athletes to get into schools through facilitating of sports Scholarship initiative. He is Nigerian, from the Igbo-speaking tribe, located in the South Eastern Region. A father of three children: Sopuluchukwu, Mesomachukwu and Adaeze, with his wife, Magdalene. He is also a distinguished Ambassador of Hope with The Global Movement of Hope and an avid believer of the gospel of Jesus Christ, and a living testimony of the magnificent work of Yahweh Elohim!

Amb. Chukwuemeka Innocent Amadi LinkedIn:

www.linkedin.com/in/amadi-chukwuemeka-a34356134

Email: affam.africanmission@gmail.com

Phone: +2348061571662

EVERY PERSON WE KILLED, IT WAS BECAUSE I SAID IT WAS OKAY

By Erika Andresen

In the early stages of my military career, when people found out I was in the Army, they would say, "Thank you for your service!" It would always make me feel uncomfortable. I was just a JAG (judge advocate, aka lawyer), so what did I really do?

That changed in 2014. I was tailgating prior to an SEC football game, and one of the senior-level coeds was introduced to me as someone who loves to debate. She asked what I did: I was a lawyer for the Army. Another girl said, "Ohhhhh, debate her!" She was full of ideals and had a yen for justice. When I challenged her by asking what she was going to do to effectuate change, she responded angrily by yelling, "Well, what have you ever done to make an impact?" Mind you, she was 21, and I was 35 at the time. I yelled back, "I took a $ 70,000-a-year salary cut and joined the fucking Army!"

And in my head, I thought, "You are welcome for my service!" I no longer felt strange having people thank me for my service. But my relationship with that phrase changed after I was deployed.

My time in Afghanistan was characterized by doing the "sexy" work – doing operational law, which is as sexy as it gets for JAG. That encompassed principles of humanitarian law, Geneva Conventions, and the law of armed conflict, as well as NATO and US tactical guidance/rules of engagement. It was interesting being in a room for 12+ hours a day, watching a giant screen with real-time video feeds of the battlefield below. Our mission in Afghanistan had changed over the years, from offensive-heavy to advising and assisting the Afghan National Army, taking a backseat, if you will.

Only when certain conditions were met could we take a more active role. A lot of people were on their 3rd, 4th, or even 7th deployment. This change of tact was difficult for some. When it came time, I had to quell what can be best described as blood lust in the room – people gearing up for a fight that might not need to happen, but it was different than every other part of the perpetual Groundhog's Day that deployments become. I alone stood between the General ordering an attack and us doing nothing.

My first strike was one that we wound up calling off. Details are not necessary other than to say that it was called off because, after watching them for a longer time than planned, thanks to a vital computer system being down, we determined they were just civilians. We came incredibly close to killing people that did not need to be killed. I came incredibly close to being responsible for the deaths of people who did not deserve to die. There is no amount of training or simulations that can prepare you for how that feels. It did not stop me, however, from approving multiple other strikes. I did my job, and I did it well the 50-odd more times I said "ok."

When it came time to go home, I had been looking forward to two things: feeling my feet bare in the grass and getting a pedicure. Feet in boots all day and lots of brown dirt – that was a daily occurrence in my deployment. Once back, my first order of business the morning I woke up: walk in the yard with my shoes off and call the nail salon two blocks away for an appointment. I called while walking in the grass. They were going to be booked all day, but if I could get there in 10 minutes, she could take me. "Great! I can be there in 5!" I grabbed my flipflops, wallet and car keys and went right over. I walked in and saw a woman starting a pedicure on a customer. She asked if she could help me. I said, "Yes, I just called about the appointment! I'm here!" She looked at the customer with her feet in the tub, who looked at me with a hand-caught-in-the-cookie-jar expression. She said, "When she walked in, I asked her if she was the woman who just called, and she said she was." I am not proud of what happened next.

My head was filled with a slew of ideas. How extraordinarily rude it is to blatantly lie to steal an appointment. How entitled this woman was. How much this woman was going to ruin my return. How I was not going to be able to get a pedicure. How she has no idea what I had just come home from. How she did not appreciate the new psychological scars I had from not only saying it was ok to kill people but watching it happen. Then I let her know everything I thought about her, screaming words that would make Martin Scorsese blush. The fact she did not apologize made me more incensed. The woman who ran the salon said she would do us both at the same time because she felt terrible about what was happening. I sat in the seat next to the appointment stealer. I was glad I made her uncomfortable because she awkwardly and silently stared at her magazine the rest of the time.

A few days later, I went to a July 4th barbeque. I showed up with my then-boyfriend at his friend's house. I knew a few of his closest friends, and they all greeted me with a "welcome back!" But I didn't feel right. I felt off. I felt like I didn't fit. That conversation was forced. What I did talk about; no one was interested in what I had to say. That no one really cared I was there. It didn't take long for me to go off and sit by myself until it was time to leave. I felt better alone, but I really wanted to not just be off to the side; I wanted to be around no one. That feeling didn't leave for a while.

I had issues connecting with my boyfriend. They call it "re-integration." I didn't tell him that there was a ceremony when we landed – I retrieved my car and drove to his place when we were released, so, in effect, I had no one to greet me when I came back. After being gone for months, we didn't have sex for at least a week. My disconnect wasn't just with him; I was doing a fund-raiser stadium climb a few weeks later. I am a chatty person by nature, and when talking to people before the start of the event, "what do you do?" came up. I said I was in the Army and had just come back from Afghanistan. I was thanked for my service and asked what that was like. I said, "You know, it was weird. I prosecuted child porn and had to watch it, but that didn't mess me up. Every person we killed was because I said it was okay. That messed me up." It got awkward. After that, I went to the Division psychiatrist to try to "fix" what I felt.

A few months of seeing the psychiatrist was beneficial to a point. I talked with a friend whose husband was a black hawk pilot for an elite unit. I mentioned to her that I felt like a fraud feeling the way I did because it wasn't as bad as someone in the infantry. She told me to stop it – that her husband felt similarly; he and I both downplayed what we did/were a part of, and we had no business doing that to ourselves. That struck me, although I didn't agree.

I moved to a new duty station and had a completely different job: ethics counsellor to a general. It was mostly about conflicts of interest with appearances with members of the public. Easy, right? I had no problem saying "thank you" to people – and there were plenty – who thanked me for my service as I was in a city that was predominately civilian. One time on a work flight back from DC, my seatmate asked what I did for the Army and where I had been. I had already been trying to sign pos that I wasn't interested in talking as I had a magazine open and kept looking at it as he was talking to me. I gave a short answer with minimal details: I was a lawyer and listed the states I lived in courtesy of the military, and I also threw in Afghanistan. "A lawyer? In Afghanistan?? What the heck do we need lawyers in Afghanistan for??" Then I got mad. I felt obligated to educate him, to irradicate his indignation. I started off with those who didn't do the "sexy" jobs. Then it came to my job: Every person we killed, it was because I said it was okay. That was now my pocket phrase to sum up, what I did in 12 words. I did get a strange satisfaction from how uncomfortable it would make people feel to hear it ... because it was uncomfortable to live with it.

I came back to thinking about being thanked for my service. I began to think about how I used to think of myself as unworthy of that sentiment because I was merely a lawyer, and people did a lot more than I did. Now I had people who thought the same way I used to think and confronted me with it. I happened to have a first date with a guy while I was in the midst of my quandary, and he started off by very genuinely thanking me for my service. I said, "You know, that's a funny phrase. People don't truly understand what that means or what the expectations are for someone who isn't an infantry member. I got to engage heavily with the scum of the earth when I prosecuted sex assaults, domestic violence, and child porn ... where I had to watch it to make a sentencing argument. As terrible as that experience was, which I had to do more than once, I also got to go to Afghanistan, and every person we killed, was because I said it was okay. People don't normally get to walk around being responsible for death. But here I am." What a way to start a date.

When it was time to leave active duty, I knew the way I responded to people about my service was (what I called) "inappropriate." I realized I probably had some PTSD surrounding my experience. Having been evaluated for and diagnosed with PTSD since leaving meant that I was able to get treatment for things I shoved down and never talked about. I discovered some of the things I struggled with related to my experience was minimizing it (which told me I had no right to feel the way I did). I also felt: I was not appreciated for what I had to endure; I don't fit (still); no one can relate to me unless they've done the same thing; I won't be liked if they know what I did; I'm a terrible person because I was good at my job.

That last one is the one I want to concentrate on. I realized through treatment that being good at my job means I am proficient at the law and can divorce emotion from my decisions to do what is best for the enterprise at the end of the day. I can kill people. Out of context, this makes me look like an evil person. In context, it means I see the whole team being impacted, not just one person. I keep the greater good of the organization in mind, but that is so long as a beneficial end is in sight. There is merit in that.

I do not compare my struggle to anyone else's struggle. I know what I feel is real. I know it was hard. I have learned not to mind-read or engage in predictions about what others will think – I will give them a fair chance. The record-scratching or blood-curdling scream from the horror of my revelation has never happened; I just assumed it would. I free myself from a prison I created and a punishment I inflicted upon myself.

Through all the intensive therapy I've been lucky to experience since getting out, I have been able to work through a lot of my issues. Solved them? That wasn't ever possible since PTSD and trauma are things I, or any of us, will have to live with. I learned I will ebb and flow with progress. Recently I was speaking with a friend, and he was genuinely happy to see me and asked what I had been up to. In my list of things that were "new with me," I mentioned I was getting intensive therapy for PTSD. He scoffed. "PTSD?? What would you have PTSD from??" Hearing that hurt. A lot. I was back again in a place of anger, in a place where I felt I had to justify that I was more than "just a lawyer." But I kept my cool. I simply said, "That's a very personal question. You know, hand-to-hand combat isn't the only thing that would give you PTSD. That's a very myopic view." Not a single swear word left my lips. I didn't even raise my voice. I understood he had limited experience with PTSD and relied on the TV shows and movies to inform his definition of military-related PTSD is: reserved for infantrymen who directly kill in close combat.

I do not regard my reaction as a failure of my therapy. It does not mean I am damaged. I found comfort in reading *The Body Keeps the Score* by Besser Van Der Kolk. One observation stood out: the author stated that he was amazed at how strong the will to live is in people who have PTSD or suffered trauma. We keep on going. We fight the ugly thoughts – not always winning, but we fight. It took reading that book and my therapists to point out my deep well of resilience. If you are reading this, you have that will … you, too, have that resilience.

Every person we killed, it was because I said it was okay. I also did a lot more than that. In all, I served my country proudly. And that is more than okay.

The one word of inspiration I would like to share is "Worthy."

"I am not worthy" is a lie we tell ourselves, especially if we've had a trauma experience. We beat ourselves up. We are not worthy of love, happiness, joy, forgiveness, good things, etc. But we are. We are worthy of all of those things, especially worthy of being healed. It took me years to figure that out, and all the help in the world won't work if you don't believe you are worthy of being the amazing, complex, and strong person you are.

"You were given this life because you are strong enough to live it." - Unknown

Erika Andresen

Erika Andresen is a business continuity expert, book author, business owner, and lecturer. She has also been an attorney with more than 16 years of experience, 8.5 of those recent years in public service as an Active Duty officer with the U.S. Army Judge Advocate General Corps. Erika initially worked in corporate law but made the transition to the military after being inspired by doing pro bono work for Veterans. Erika spent her Active Duty career advising Generals in both garrison and while deployed in Afghanistan, as well as Soldiers individually and their commanders. During her Active Duty time, Ms. Andresen spent the majority of her career working on legal issues surrounding foreign and domestic threats (natural and man-made) and established an authoritative presence at training exercises. Erika transitioned from Active Duty to the reserves for the last two years. She is proud to be a decorated Veteran, community volunteer and advocate for mental health.

To contact Erika Andresen:

www.eaasc.com

WHY DOES HOPE MATTER?

By Manjit Kaur

Our lives are laden with myriad possibilities, some good, some not-so-good and some bone-chillingly dreadful. We remain vulnerable to this sense of the unpredictable that does not allow us to take anything much for granted. Yet most of us aspire to live full and rich lives and make the most of our live's experiences.

Despite the good, the not-so-good, and the chillingly dreadful that life sometimes throws at us unpredictably; we forge our individual paths as best as we can.

What drives us forward is HOPE – hope for the silver lining behind every cloud, for light at the end of the tunnel, and for circumstances to improve, no matter how bleak things are in the here and the now.

According to Hope Researcher C.R.Synder, hope gives us the possibility of a better tomorrow and keeps us going, and propels us forward, especially when things are difficult. He described hope as follows:

"A rainbow is a prism that sends shards of multicoloured light in various directions. It lifts our spirits and makes us think of what is possible. Hope is the same – a personal rainbow of the mind."

Synder's Hope Theory defines hope as life-sustaining strength that comprises three critical aspects: goals thinking, which is the ability to clearly conceptualize valuable goals; pathways thinking, which is the ability to develop specific strategies to realize those goals; and agency thinking, which is the ability to initiate and sustain the motivation required to implement the specific strategies to reach those goals.

Barbara Fredrickson, a positive psychology researcher, describes hope as the glimmer that *"opens us up,"* strengthens our resolve and turns us towards something better. Psychologist Dacher Keltner's research links the feeling of being awe-stricken by something that is so important to us that it moves us and fills us with a sense of hopefulness, inspiration and deep connection.

Research on hope tells us that hope helps us to better manage stress and acts as a protective factor against chronic anxiety. It provides us with the necessary coping mechanism to deal with adversity and helps to build endurance and resilience. Interestingly, it is also found to protect us against perceptions of vulnerability, uncontrollability, and unpredictability.

The research also collectively points to how hope motivates us to take positive action, serves as a pathway from one stage to the next, and moves us toward our goals in meaningful ways. It helps us take on healthier perspectives and enhances our optimism. It is also linked to better academic and athletic performance, improved physical and psychological well-being, better self-esteem and interpersonal relationships.

All these factors contribute to hope being positively related to overall life satisfaction, with an emphasis on positive involvement and engagement in healthy behaviour, despite challenges and limitations.

While we can all agree that hope contributes to our well-being, how can we incorporate hope in healthy and grounded doses into our personal lives? Positive psychology, which focuses on building and enhancing well-being, propagates a host of hope therapy techniques that include practicing gratitude, positive self-talk, engaging in acts of kindness, practicing mindfulness and staying in the present moment, stepping out of comfort zones and creating new ways of thinking, practicing creative visualizations and connecting with support networks, among others. These are some examples of hope-based interventions designed to improve well-being.

Awareness of the importance of hope is growing, as evidenced by the work being done at the Hope Studies Central, which is a research unit dedicated to the study and research of hope in our lives for the past 30 years.

It's highly likely that we may all have come across inspiring examples of hope triumphing over adversity, perhaps in our own lives. We may not be fully aware of this, but if we look closely enough, we may be able to spot life events when hope helped us navigate and overcome, and perhaps even survive, challenging situations. Such retrospective examinations of past events may throw up powerful life lessons for us from our own lives.

When I look back at the way I have personally dealt with adversity in the past, common trends emerge that all point to building upon hope.

As the eldest child in the family, when my late father passed on when we were all still very young, and left me with the responsibility of taking care of my younger siblings and my mother, it was hope for a better tomorrow that propelled me forward.

And I did manage to educate all my siblings and myself in the process. It was not easy, but hope and the belief that there's always a way kept me going. Today, I count this as my greatest character-building experience and among my greatest achievements.

Life has thrown many other curve balls in my direction since. Each time I felt my optimism was being impacted negatively, I would look at past gains and restore my faith in myself and in my hope that things would generally get better. And they always do.

I have also found practicing creative visualization and meditation to be extremely useful. These techniques have helped me to sharpen my focus and build upon positive experiences while always sustaining hope for positive outcomes.

When I was a struggling single parent to my daughter, and I wrestled with self-doubt over my ability to balance my career and my parenting abilities, I found out, quite by accident, that cheering for myself, in grounded and realistic ways, helped me to significantly boost my self-confidence and resilience during all those years.

It helped me to focus on and build upon what I was doing well and doing right. This was a more meaningful approach as it was future-oriented and helped me steer clear from negative and meaningless agony and despair over the whole situation.

My experiences continue to teach me that confidence and hope are closely woven together. I am now happily remarried, and my daughter has turned out to be a most lovely, intelligent and gracious young lady. I believe wholeheartedly that hope sustained me throughout all those years.

I have also learned to respect and appreciate setbacks. When I find myself going off-tangent in working towards my goals, I make it a point to reassess the whole situation and recalibrate accordingly and as necessary while trying to steer clear of going into either the "blaming others" or "shaming myself" modes.

I also make it a point to celebrate whatever progress I make – however little. I have found this approach to be especially helpful in keeping alive my belief in my goals and my hope of attaining them.

I lost my mother recently. Throughout her two weeks of hospital stay and another two weeks of home-based palliative care, what sustained me was hope that her transition and pathway to her next stage of being would be comfortable and smooth and would grant her peace. This hope helped me cope with the grief of losing her.

My favourite quote on hope is from the Dalai Lama:

"Optimism doesn't mean that you are blind to the reality of the situation. It means that you remain motivated to seek a solution to whatever problems arise."

Hope therefore provides us with healthier perspectives and more optimistic outlooks so that we can take more meaningful, positive and future-oriented action, despite the most challenging circumstances.

Manjit Kaur

Manjit is a business entrepreneur and a Positive Psychology practitioner who focuses on business, team and leadership excellence as well as people development.

Manjit Kaur, Singapore

Email: manjit@mysuccessmind.com

Born To Grow or Growing Into the Miracle You Are

By Jason W. Freeman

I find it all too easy to take the miracle of growth for granted. I grew from a few cells in my momma to where I am now, typing this on my laptop. Likewise, you grew from a few cells in your mother to where you are now, reading this article. That's all magnificent and miraculous, and yet so typical because growth is not only the story of our own lives but the story of the lives of everyone around us.

Indeed, one of the secrets to understanding the successful person I've grown into is that I wasn't born successful. In fact, I was so excited to get into the world that I came a few weeks early and surprised my folks in the middle of the night. It wasn't the best idea because they were sleeping, but luckily they both had very clear heads and got us to the emergency room in time.

However, in the process, my umbilical cord became kinked like a garden hose, and I lost some oxygen. As a result, I have a pronounced speech impediment and some coordination differences. Definitely not the typical beginning of a biography of a successful speaker and coach.

We can easily begin to take the miracle of who we've grown into for granted. Heck, it's a miracle I survived my birth. Think for a minute about how many fortunate things have happened in your life that have allowed you to grow into who you are today. Think of the challenges you've been through.

We often think of where we are now, not in terms of where we've come from since we were born, but rather how we perceive our lives at the moment compared to all we yet want to accomplish.

For instance, I'm at the point in my career where there's a great deal on my CV that I'm proud of: a TEDx talk, over 100 speaking engagements, a book, clients who've had breakthroughs, a network of colleagues in the speaking and coaching industry, and a podcast with more than 100 fifty episodes and a wide range of guests from business leaders to a Canadian Olympian.

Basically, I inspire people to do their imperfect best to live the most vibrant life they can envision for themselves. Even after all that, on many occasions, I still tend to slip into thinking of all I haven't accomplished yet.

To get to this point in my career, I had to grow out of my seventh-grade habit of severely tormenting myself. (Who, like me, is glad that we've grown beyond how we felt about ourselves as preteens and teenagers?) Back then, I hated the sound of my voice and hated that I tended to catch basketballs with basically any part of my body other than my hands.

I hated that I was constantly scared and stressed about things in the news that I had no idea how to positively impact. I had so much hatred within me that I attempted to take my own life in the spring of seventh grade. Fortunately, my heart still wanted to grow, so I called for help.

Even after surviving myself in seventh grade and accomplishing all that I have, I tend to slip into thinking of all I haven't achieved yet.

To go from my suicide attempt when I was so young to filling up my CV with accomplishments is indeed exponential growth. But instead of feeling good about this growth, how often do I feel mopey because I haven't yet come anywhere close to making my first million, not to mention my tenth or twentieth million?

I tell you all this because before you think of the challenges you want to navigate in the future and the dreams you desire to realize, I want you to reflect on the capacity to grow that you've already demonstrated. You've grown through a myriad of challenges, from learning to walk to the biggest challenge you have faced and journeyed through. It is part of who you are.

Indeed, you come to the challenges you currently face and the dreams you want to create with a great deal of experience in being able to grow and learn new skills.

We all have challenges that we have the opportunity to struggle with. At least until we learn to calmly work through them, so we can either grow out of them or grow with them.

About twelve years ago, I had an opportunity to speak to an audience. I was heartened not only by how much my message resonated with them and how uplifted they felt but also by the feeling of joy I received when I spoke to them. On that day, I became highly energized with the dream of developing my own business as a professional speaker.

When I went into business for myself, I figured I had to make a ton of money fast to prove the worth of my dream, but an eight-month-old doesn't ask herself, "How much will my earning potential expand if I learn to walk?" She just has the dream that she wants to walk, so she devotes herself to the purpose of learning to walk.

I believe we humans are meant not only to grow older but to do our imperfect best to practice growing in our abilities as we age. Always remember we grow through achievement, but we can also grow out of pain. When I started my business, I had very, very lean years. It often felt like what I was doing wasn't helping, that I was doing nothing and that my business would never improve. But during those years, even though I was practically oblivious to it, I was learning the skills it would take to have better years.

I strive to grow every day in my capacity to be exactly who I am and to offer exactly what I'm on this Earth to offer. I'm very much a work in progress, but the more I engage in disciplines of mindfulness, organization, and action-taking, the more my life expands, and the more people I'm able to inspire.

My favourite word of inspiration is actually two words-"Imperfect Best." I choose "Imperfect Best" because as humans, we have the power to dream big and strive for the best we envision. "a best" we can only currently see in our dreams.

We are human, so mistakes, roadblocks, frustrations, confusion will come up as we strive for our 'this best.' Instead of using these "Imperfections" as a reason to stop, "doing our imperfect best" invites us to learn from these "imperfections" and continue to move forward.

It is the philosophy of using all the imperfections of life as learning opportunities and inspiration to move forward toward the best we envision.

I find this quote by Marianne Williamson tremendously inspiring.

"Our deepest fear is not that we are inadequate. Our deepest fear is that we are powerful beyond measure. It is our light, not our darkness that most frightens us. We ask ourselves, 'Who am I to be brilliant, gorgeous, talented, fabulous?' Actually, who are you not to be? You are a child of God. Your playing small does not serve the world. There is nothing enlightened about shrinking so that other people won't feel insecure around you. We are all meant to shine, as children do. We were born to make manifest the glory of God that is within us. It's not just in some of us; it's in everyone. And as we let our own light shine, we unconsciously give other people permission to do the same. As we are liberated from our own fear, our presence automatically liberates others."

Jason W. Freeman

Whenever Jason Freeman speaks to an audience, be it an intimate mastermind in North County San Diego or an assembly of 1,500 high school students in Austin, Minnesota, he is absolutely, 100% committed to bringing his speech impediment with him. Jason has a unique walk, a love for country music, a sweet tooth, a Master of Fine Arts in Poetry, a TEDx Talk and a book he authored called *"Awkwardly Awesome: Embracing My Imperfect Best."* His goal is to speak to millions of people in his lifetime.

Jason Freeman

https://jasonwfreeman.com

TEDx Talk: https://youtu.be/HCu5IIibe20

Phone - 1-619-823-8536

Facebook: https://m.facebook.com/mrjasonwfreeman/

LinkedIn:https://www.linkedin.com/in/jason-w-freeman-72150944/

Twitter: @JasonFreemanYES

WHEN I WAS GIVEN 5 YEARS TO LIVE

By Leanne Kabat

Turning 50 is a milestone for most people, but for me, it was everything. It was a number I had dreamt about every day for 15 years, hoping to see, praying to reach.

In March 2006, our little family moved from Canada to the U.S., and soon after, my husband went on a business trip, leaving me in our new home in our new city with our kids.

Waking up in the middle of the night felt like one of those times when you forget who you are and where you are, and what year you're in. I was groggy and confused, but the gentle breath of my daughter on my right arm brought me right back. I was in her bed. Her little 2-year-old body pressed right up against me, creating this heat bond that was rivalled only by the heat between me and my 4-year-old on the other side. All three of us were squeezed into her twin bed. No, actually, all four of us. I was five months pregnant.

I had to use the bathroom. I looked at the clock; it was just after 2:00 a.m. With the stealth of an elephant in a glass museum, I disentangled my arms and legs from theirs and maneuvered my bulging body over the side of her bed. My first foot hit the floor with a small tap, and I was almost free. My second leg was caught in the pink and yellow quilt, but when I shook it free, I smiled that they stayed asleep. When my foot touched the ground, and I turned to leave her room, I blacked out and fell to the floor. My brain came back online quickly.

What happened?

I fainted and collapsed.

Did I trip on the blanket?

No, I was free from it, so that wasn't it.

So why am I still lying on this cold floor?

I don't really know.

Wait, where are the kids?

Sleeping. I can hear them.

Why can't I get off the floor?

   I can't move.

Why can't my arms push me up?

I'm trying. Seriously, I can't get up. Oh no, I'm on the baby. All my weight is on my belly. I need to get up. Leanne, get up. GET UP! Please let me up. Please, someone, help me up. LET ME UP! I'll do anything. I'll be a better mother, wife, sister, daughter, friend, cousin, helper. I'll do anything you need. PLLLLEEEAAASSSEEEEEEE.

For five hours, I felt waves of terror, rage, and fear. Five hours of silently begging, pleading, negotiating, asking, crying, demanding, forcing, and finally surrendering.

In order to fully surrender, I had to find a way to calm down, but it was so hard. In the quiet of the bedroom, I used the rhythm of their breathing to be the drumbeats of my breathing, and I calmed myself like infants regulate to their mother's heartbeat.

Even though my panic had subsided a bit, I kept imagining their confusion and fear when they woke up and saw me on the floor, in a puddle of pee and tears, unable to move. I kept breathing.

Sometime after seven, things started to change. The heat came first, starting in my belly and working its way through my core and up to my head. Pink neon flashes zipped across my eyes. My mouth tasted like metal and old spit. The spinning was so intense I pushed harder into the floor so I wouldn't fall. Oh, the irony.

I stood up and went to the bathroom; then I changed my clothes. I woke the kids, made them breakfast; then I told them we were going for a ride. We hopped in the car, and I typed 'hospital' into our car's GPS since we didn't know where it was in our new city, and we raced to get some answers.

The first and only question on my mind was if the baby was okay since I was on my stomach for hours. A quick ultrasound showed the baby was perfectly fine, yet we were shuffled from room to room throughout the day in a search for answers.

When we left late into the night, no one had any idea what had happened to me. All the doctors insisted my collapse was a one-time thing, and with a pat on the back, they sent us home. Right away, strange things started happening to me and I knew I wasn't fine.

Over the next few months, I saw dozens of doctors in different specialties with the hope that they would be able to solve the puzzle of what happened, and what kept happening to my body.

In the midst of all of this uncertainty, one glorious, brilliant, bright light appeared to remind us that we could be certain about one thing for sure: love is powerful. The day our son was born was the greatest day because after months of secretly worrying the doctors were wrong, I could see for myself that my baby was healthy and strong.

My mama heart was relieved, but my body was getting weaker and sicker. The testing intensified, and I endured even more poking, prodding, scanning, and screenings on my quest.

Finally, in November, my doctor called me to come in to hear the results of all the tests since the first incident in March.

MRI scans of my brain and body were displayed on the light box, and my lab results covered the table. I was excited that within all these images and numbers, I would have answers. There were two doctors present in our meeting, and they looked at me kindly. After going over each test individually, they looked at each other and looked down.

My primary care doctor spoke next and very softly. "Your brain is not working the way it should because there's something hurting you from the inside. The scans show us that you have suffered brain damage in some areas of your brain that will impact you in your daily life, and you have a very high risk of stroke. We are so sorry. We don't know what it is, but based on everything we see, we know it's going to kill you."

"What? When?" I shrieked.

5 years.

"This Thursday is Thanksgiving, and it's my birthday. Are you saying after this week, I'll only have four more birthdays and four more Thanksgivings with my family?"

"What we are saying is we want you to go home, Leanne, love your children, live your life, and get your affairs in order."

I left that appointment in a fog of anger and confusion. What were they talking about? I had three small children at home, and we were going to celebrate both holidays together, and our little family was going to play games and colour pictures and watch movies.

It felt like my heart had been squeezed so tightly in my chest it might stop pumping. I gasped for air and started to cry. When the last tear fell, I wiped my face and drove home, pretending nothing had happened.

For the first few years, I was very busy dying. Every medication and treatment pushed me deeper into a zombie-like fog, and I struggled to be a decent mother, let alone a good one. I couldn't run and play, I couldn't create fun games or bake cookies in the shapes of animals, and I couldn't be the 'class parent' the school wanted me to be.

And my illness didn't just affect my parenting. I couldn't be the wife I wanted to be, or sister, or daughter, or friend. Who I had become was so far from who I wanted to be I felt like a failure before my eyes opened each day.

On top of my own internal emotional storm, there were external reminders of my five-year-to-live deadline everywhere: I saw the number 5 — at the gas station, on the price tags at the grocery store, on the clock, and even in the phone number on the van idling beside me in traffic.

I couldn't escape the feeling that the universe was mocking me, and I was powerless against it. I became a woman who turned on the shower to hide her sobs, who let her bangs grow long to hide her swollen, puffy eyes. I was barely living.

At one of my annual appointments, my neurologist casually asked if there was anything I was hoping to do while I was healthy enough to do it. The question caught me off guard as we never talked about things outside of symptoms and test results anymore, but without any delay, I had my answer. Like millions of people, I had always fantasized about travelling the world when I was older, visiting festive European Christmas markets and feeling the silky sand beaches of tropical islands in the south Pacific Ocean, climbing the tallest mountains and swimming in the deepest seas.

With my condition, I no longer had the luxury of growing old so I blurted out, "I'm going to travel to 50 countries before I turn 50."

She laughed nervously and then stopped, looking at me sternly. "If you're serious, then you better start today."

"Can I really do it?" I asked.

"Do you really want it?" She questioned.

"I'm not going to live long enough to give my kids the world, but I can show it to them. Yes, I really want it. I want it for me, for them, and for our family as a whole."

The number five haunted me, but the number fifty rescued me. From that moment on, every penny we had and every minute of free time I found in our calendar went to travelling. I bought a giant map and started to plan how we could make this happen for five people on one salary.

We kept our packing to a bare minimum so we could fit in one car or get on and off trains and subways easily. We travelled off-season on flights no one else wanted, typically red-eyes and those with long layovers, but we loved those the most because flying overnight saved us a night at a hotel, and we were always able to extend our layovers a day or two to visit new places without making a big time commitment.

We rented cheap apartments instead of hotels so we could spread out and have a kitchen to cut down on food costs. We found all the free things to do in each city, only paying for things we really wanted to experience, like climbing the Eiffel Tower or sailing through the islands in Belize.

Over the next few years, we visited places many people go, like Australia, France, and Italy, and places fewer people go, like Estonia, Vanuatu, and Montenegro. Our destinations were driven by the deals I could find to have the best experiences, make the best memories, and see the most of this glorious planet with my kids.

When we were travelling, we were completely happy, enjoying all the sights, sounds, and surprises we encountered, but I always had a mental countdown for the number of days until my 40th birthday when my life was going to end.

Wherever we were, I pushed through the pain, tried to cover up my condition and give my family memories to last their lifetime. Even though every day I worried that 'this is the headache that precedes the fatal stroke,' or 'this is the symptom that signals the end is near,' I never stopped bringing our family on the next adventure.

Then, something miraculous happened. I woke up on the day of my 40th birthday, the day after that, and the day after that. I was ecstatic that maybe the doctors were wrong, and at my next appointment, I mentioned that to my team.

They told me it doesn't work that way; my condition was permanent. My doctor put my latest brain scan up on the lightbox and told me what she saw, the deterioration and the decline. A spark ignited in me, and for the first time, I pushed back.

"My scans show many things, but do you know what they don't show? How happy I am to jump over the waves with my kids, and how fun it is to try flavours of ice cream we've never heard of before, scrub a baby elephant, or hike through the jungle looking at bugs we've only seen in books.

They don't show that I am more alive than I've ever been, and I'm fighting like hell to keep it that way."

She told me she didn't have another patient who was fighting as fiercely as I was, and she was honoured to watch me live so fully. She cried, I cried, and we hugged for a very long time.

In January 2020, we were able to spend the holidays in the Philippines. It was country 49, and I had big plans for country 50. However, everything changed in March with the start of the catastrophic pandemic, and we didn't leave our neighbourhood for over a year. Like billions of other people, we stayed home, we relived our travels through pictures and memories, and we dreamed some new dreams.

My 50th birthday was coming up in November 2021, and I was so proud of what I had accomplished in my travels, in my life goals, and in my small business, even though I didn't reach my goal of fifty countries.

Then, two weeks before my birthday, we had a chance to travel somewhere new. We discussed it with the tour company in the country for days. Is it safe? Is it wise? Is it respectful of the host country to have foreign visitors? They assured us it was the perfect time and the perfect way to support people who rely on tourism to live.

We dutifully followed all health protocols, were up to date on all our immunizations, and my husband and I kissed our kids, now 20, 18, and 15. We packed a small bag and raced like kids at Disneyland to visit Jordan and the United Arab Emirates. It was magical and magnificent, and I was in constant awe that we were trekking the desert on camelback, riding to the top of the tallest tower in the world, and touching the holiest waters in the world.

Even though I fell sick for three days in a foreign land, I would do it all over again because not every goal is reached with glitter and gold. Some goals are met by dragging yourself across the finish line, and that's perfectly ok.

It's fun to dream, but we have to be honest: no one makes it through this life without hardship.

The storms will always come. You don't have the medical condition I have, but you have your own challenges, maybe with your health, your family, your finances, or your future. Maybe your trauma has kept you trapped for days, months, or decades. Maybe you don't have the resources to build the life of your dreams yet, or you don't believe you even could. I get it.

I didn't think I had any power to overcome the prognosis from a team of top medical experts, but somehow, I found just enough power each day to carry me through.

You don't have to do everything today, just one thing, even a tiny thing, to move you in the direction of your dreams.

None of us are getting out alive. I've just happened to face it much earlier than most, and it has become a part of me, my worldview and my life force and life fuel.

For every day, every opportunity, or every experience, we all hold the same one coin. It can be a curse or a gift, it just depends on which side of the coin you are looking at. For me, I have a degenerative brain condition, and it is definitely both a curse and a gift.

It's a curse because I live each day fretfully, on borrowed time.

It's a gift because I live each day fully, on borrowed time.

It's a curse because it reminds me I don't have long.

It's a gift because it reminds me I don't have long.

It's a curse because there's something so wrong with me.

It's a gift because there's something so right with me.

What is so right today is I am alive.

And I would not have done so much living if I wasn't told I was dying.

I will never know if I would have died before 2011 if I didn't have a big, juicy, delicious goal like travelling to 50 countries. But I know that having a goal like this gave me hope, put my attention on things other than my illness, and helped me live a life I love, so even if it ended prematurely, I didn't wait to live.

I often think about the meme that says I don't want to arrive at my gravesite in pristine condition, with my hair neatly done and my nails perfectly manicured. I want to slide into it with all of me tattered and torn, dishevelled and undone, coming from a magnificently wild life.

Live wild, my friends, set big goals, and put you first, for being your best self is the best gift for everyone around you.

I wish you the courage to do everything you can to reach your potential, to become the best you are meant to be. Your life is waiting for you to live it fully, and don't be afraid to become dishevelled and undone along the way.

My one word of inspiration is:

Choose

Before we can renew and rejuvenate, before we can grow and transform, before we can create and accomplish, we must choose. It took many years to really believe that even on my darkest days, in my saddest moments, I had the power of choice.

I could choose a shower or a snack; I could choose a movie or music; I could choose to call a friend or call it a day. Our true power grows stronger every time we choose things that heal our hearts, feed our souls, and lets us be in our brilliance, whatever that is for each of us.

"Our greatest glory is not in never falling, but in rising every time we fall." -Oliver Goldsmith (some say Confucious was the author, but this is the source I used to authenticate: Our Greatest Glory Is Not in Never Falling, But in Rising Every Time We Fall – Quote Investigator)

We all face obstacles and challenges in our lives that knock us down, take us out, or push us to our edge. We can't stop the storms from coming into our lives, but we can get up each time to nurture love, growth, expansion, and abundance.

Leanne Kabat

Leanne Kabat is an international speaker and the author of 'The 5 Seasons of Connection' collection. Her life-changing philosophy takes us right into those crucial minute-by-minute interactions, where we either draw closer together or push further apart. By understanding our seasons, we can transform every relationship from conflicted to connected, confidently moving out of the dark, stormy Winter times towards love, happiness, and sunny Summer days.

Her first book helps overwhelmed parents connect on a deeper level with their kids, her second book explores the most profound adult relationship we have, guiding couples out of Winter and towards their deepest love and most intimate connection, and her third book helps entrepreneurs overcome fears of success and failure to build a profitable business on their brilliance. She has taught her 5 Seasons framework to families, couples, and entrepreneurs in dozens of countries, including Uganda, the Philippines, Austria, Australia, South Africa, Canada, and the U.S.

Leanne developed the 5 Seasons framework after she received a medical diagnosis in 2006 that gave her five years to live, challenging her to truly live a life she loved, including setting a super-ambitious goal of visiting fifty countries before she turned fifty. Over fifteen years later, she's grateful to witness her children become incredible adults, and when they aren't travelling, they love to reminisce about the powerful life lessons they have learned on their adventures around the world. Leanne successfully reached her big travel goal and is excited to explore country #54 when it's safe to do so.

Leanne Kabat

LinkedIn: www.linkedin.com/in/leannekabat

HOPE AS THE TREE OF LIFE

"Oxygen helps you survive....and hope gives you purpose to live" -

By MD Samir Hasan

I think hope plays the role of a tree in everyone's life. A tree plays an extremely important role in our life and we we enjoy many benefits from it as every life especially requires oxygen to survive. Without oxygen, it is impossible to live and is that oxygen which is provided to us by trees. Not only oxygen, but trees also give us many other things, such as beauty, it bears delicious food and fruits with seeds, provides wood to build the necessities of life and to use as fuel to heat our homes. Trees also provide shade, wind breaks, habitats for animals, leaves that possess healing powers, sweet perfumed trees, and incense. Similarly, hope helps a lot in the life of every human being. Hope gives us a purpose to live, teaches us to dream, helps us a lot to face the difficult situations of life with courage.

A tree is a powerful symbol of hope.

As "if a tree is cut down, there is "hope" that it will grow again and will send out new branches." Even if its deep roots grow old in the ground, and its stump dies in the dirt, at the onset of water, it will bud out new shoots and life. Hope is like the tree of life even where life fails to appear to exist, Hope endures with possibility and is the light in the darkness. It comes as no surprise, then, that in the face of tragedies of life, trees often become symbols of strength, resilience, perseverance, and deep hope. *"When we see a tree come back from the brink of destruction, it inspires us and reminds us that life goes on and we can and will find a way to also heal and grow."*

Trees, along with hope, help us become more aware of our connections with something much larger than ourselves. Hope is a gift that works together to give us confidence, joy, peace, power and love. Without hope and other virtues such as faith and love, we risk descending into despair.

In addition, hope gives us motivation and, coupled with action, plays an important role in moving us toward successfully achieving our goals. As Nadene Joy so beautifully states, "*Hope without Action is like Fire without Fuel.*" We can hope for something all day long; however, if we do not choose to "do" something about it to make a change and take action, nothing will change, and we will continue to stay in the same cycle and situation we've been in for months or even perhaps our entire life. Action fuels Hope just as wood fuels fire.

The Tree of Life also synchronistically symbolizes one's unique individuality. Trees, like each one of us and like our fingerprints, are all unique, with their branches sprouting at different points and, most times, also in completely different directions. It symbolizes a person's personal growth into a unique human being as different experiences shape us into who we are today. Remember to always honour yourself wherever you are on your personal journey as you are exactly where you are meant to be and that you will never be given anything that is too big for you to handle. Be patient and hopeful as anything is possible when you have faith and believe.

Every person in the world should live with hope. Everyone has to go through tests at different times in life and hope is the only thing that helps us to get good results in those tests. So everyone should be optimistic. There is no substitute for hope in the world.

Hope Quotes by MD Samir Hasan:

"Hope is the most precious asset in the world because it is hope that will lead you towards your goal."

"You may survive for days without food, but you cannot survive for a moment without hope."

"Hope is the thing that helps you face all the problems because you know that maybe after some time the situation will be changed."

"Hope is the power that always keeps you from committing suicide. So live every moment of life with much hope."

"Everything in the world has an alternative way, but there is no alternative to hope."

"Inspiring ourselves so we are able to inspire others: It all Starts with "You."

The one word of inspiration I would like to share is the actually the word "inspiration" itself.

For me, inspiration is a weapon to move forward. Because as you move towards your goal you will face various obstacles, dangers and problems on the way. Then this weapon called inspiration will help you to face them.

When you inspire yourself, victory is near you because inspiration will never let you lose.

Inspiration works invisibly within you which no one can see but when its work is complete, the whole world sees its results through you.

Inspiration is like a key for me. For example, a key is essential to open a locked room which cannot be entered without the key. Inspiration is the key to our success and the success of others we come in contact with, which is impossible without Inspiration.

Inspiration is the weapon that moves you forward and is one thing that will never let you down and will help you win. Sometimes in life, you have to inspire yourself. I speak here from my real experiences in life when there is no one around you and when you have to inspire yourself. Through this, you receive an unlimited strength that will help you in every area of your life. Inspiration plays an important role in each of our lives. It is the responsibility of each of us to try our best to inspire ourselves first in order to be able to inspire everyone around us so that we can build a beautiful society and a strong nation and a positive world, which will be a tremendous gift from us to our next generation and to many generations to come.

MD Samir Hasan

Samir is a 20 year-old student from Bangladesh who is the eldest son of a middle-class family. He has had various life experiences which are beyond imagination. Among them, he wants to share that he has had several dreams in his past which, even though they have not been fulfilled yet, he is not upset at all about it. He is still trying his best and very hopeful that they will be fulfilled very soon. He has faced many problems in life and struggled alone. He learned a lot from it all. In fact, he says you have to struggle to fulfill your dreams, and you can learn a lot through the struggle. He is not disappointed by this, and you are probably in a much better position than him, so never be disappointed. Always be an optimist in life, as circumstances may change at any time. Always inspire yourself. Your hope and inspiration will be your pillars of strength that will sustain you in difficult times and help a lot. Finally, he advises you to:

"Keep trying until you reach your desired goal because success is near you and is much nearer than you think."

Youth Leader of Hope

Finding your THRIVE

By Nancy Barrows

I was sexually abused by my grandfather until I was 16 years old (a mandated reporter called The Department of Family and Child Welfare because they had reason to be suspicious). In connection with that, I developed the eating disorder Anorexia, which was 'abuse-related" because I hated my body and wanted to disappear. In the midst of all of this, I experienced my first, of many, major depressive episodes while in my junior year of college after confronting my grandfather and dropping out of college. There is so much more to the story. However, I believe the value in sharing my story is in the struggle to heal and 'get healthy.' We talk about 'success' and have models of what 'getting better' and having 'healed' looks like, but very rarely do we hear the 'snotty, ugly' parts of the story. What I needed to hear during my journey were the stories about the pain, the questioning, the anger, the challenges, the days you wanted to give up, the feeling of being isolated, crying yourself to sleep, not getting out of bed for three days and being convinced that you are broken and beyond repair. I share my story in order to let people know that they are not alone in how they feel, think, react or behave in response to trauma, specifically sexual abuse/assault.

Trauma changes our brains. Being a person who has thrived after being sexually abused, I have gained a valuable set of tools, namely being willing and able, to talk about the most shameful, excruciating moments of my life, to listen understandingly to others and empower people to own and share their personal story. There are conversations that would make someone who had not been sexually abused/assaulted uncomfortable, making them difficult to have. Imagine hearing that every cell in my body was built to feel pleasure from being touched in a sexual manner, and it did just that. Pleasure during abusive episodes is part of my experience, hence my story. That alone is shocking and uncomfortable for most people to receive, but to me, it is relatable. I did not want to 'enjoy' the sexual touch of my grandfather. It felt like I betrayed myself every time, until my brain, in its brilliance, figured out that I could be outside of my body looking in to avoid all of the physical sensations I was experiencing. My mind and body got divorced, and it was not amicable. They did not talk and often battled one another, with my mind winning. I was an Olympic calibre, gold medalist, world-champion of dissociating, therefore not feeling anything. I knew how to do that; what I could not do was turn it off and connect back to my body to experience the positive. It led me to hate my body and believe that I was broken beyond repair. While I was sheltered from pain, I would never experience joy if it did not change.

How I got through it- strategies and modalities/ therapies, personal self-care practices, support systems, etc., used to help cope

I had a whole host of maladaptive behaviours, thoughts and reactions to sort through. I had basically lived my whole life with my mind detached/separated from my body. The natural, healthy sexual response of pleasure was twisted and distorted. Trust and love had been polluted. My head and my heart never talked. I could not possibly list all the issues I have processed over the years. As a fun bonus, they changed as I progressed through life. It felt never-ending. It was as if every victory brought with it a new delivery of 'stuff' to unpack, examine and therapy away. It was a moving target of 'need to heal.' I did get through, but there were many days when I did not think I could or would. On my worst days, I didn't want to 'make it.'

Therapy was one of the most powerful tools to which I had access. I was fortunate. I had a supportive family that never once asked, "Are you sure?" who 'believed' in therapy and had the means to pay for it. I acknowledge this, sadly, is not the case for everyone. I believe that without it, I would not be the person I am today. Actually, I absolutely know that, and I certainly would not be able to share my story and help others. I have been, and continue to be, in and out of therapy since I was 16 years old. It does not mean I have failed or have not healed; it means I am a human being who recognizes when she needs help and values herself enough to seek it out. I have heard many stories of people seeing a therapist and not feeling comfortable enough to tell them everything and sometimes going as far as lying to their therapist (this is not unique to sexual abuse). I am guilty of this, as well. If you are struggling with this, know it is 'normal.' It is incredibly difficult to share your deepest, darkest fears and secrets with a stranger. To expose the pieces you feel are unloveable and should be punished and considered repulsive, "airing" your shame and guilt and discovering just how much more there is, is NOT easy. HOWEVER, it is possible when you find 'your' mental health/wellness practitioner. I am sure people are wondering, "But how will I know?" You will know you have found that person because the part of you that wants to heal will scream more loudly than the part that is terrified. I can't say I know what it will be for you or that I could give you criteria to look for, but what I can do is share my experience. I have been to many therapists, but the three who 'saved' me, the three I am so deeply grateful for that it brings me to tears, are Dr. Suzanne Drake, Dr. Janine Shelby and Jessica Oifer, M.A., LMFT. They are all brilliantly talented professionals, but for me, I knew they were 'my' therapist because they let me use the therapy space in any way I desired to do so. They let me make it uniquely mine and made sure I knew that was the case.

Suzanne was the first therapist that I chose to see (I had been through court-ordered therapy a few years prior). My work with Suzanne started when I was entering my Senior year of High

School. The process was hard and arduous. I have an abundance of empathy and accolades for the young woman who walked through Suzanne's door shaking and desperate. There were foundational tools that I did not possess and needed to learn and trusted that she knew how to teach me those pieces. Mostly, I had to take the leap of faith that she would not be repulsed by my story and that she would help me begin to own it. When I first started seeing Suzanne, it felt impossible to say the words vagina and penis, much less describe what I had experienced! I used slang for the things I did not have words for in my vocabulary. I fumbled, but I got there. I do not know how it started, but I determined that the only way I could speak to Suzanne about the details of my abuse was to pull the sofa away from the wall and sit behind it where I couldn't see her, and she could not see me. That therapy space was mine. She did not comment on it or 'correct the choice.' She let me be. She even started pulling the sofa away from the wall in anticipation of my appointments. I eventually worked my way back around to the front of the sofa and could sit facing her when we talked. Win number 1 for Nancy! Even in writing this, I cry because this was the greatest gift anyone has ever given me. The knowledge that I had the ability to speak my truth face-to-face with another person. Without it, without her, and all the things she taught me and helped me 'undo', who knows where the journey would have led, but because I had Suzanne Drake Kilduff, I learned to talk about what had happened and to begin feeling the feelings. When I dropped out of college, I saw her three times a week and did group sessions. She taught me how to find my therapist and when to walk through their door. 'Thank you' does not begin to cover it, Suzanne!

I found Dr. Shelby after a particularly difficult search for a therapist. Getting myself to even call the numbers for the therapists that had been shared with me was beyond challenging, as was the telephone tag that ensued. Interviewing, meeting and deciding on a therapist was not the right fit for me — it was exhausting. Hearing people's fees left me feeling defeated. Finding a therapist who really specialized in and was trained in trauma therapy and actually had experience in treating trauma seemed impossible. I was now married, and new things kept coming up rapid fire. I needed a therapist badly. I was overwhelmed and it was impacting my relationship, my work and my functioning. In a moment of clarity, I thought to call the Santa Monica- Rape Treatment Center and shared my difficulty finding a therapist and my sense of desperation. In return, they gave me a list of names to try and no guarantee that it would pan out. Dr. Janine Shelby was first on the list and my last call. Hearing her voice on the phone, I felt it; she was my therapist. Dr. Shelby had this amazing Zen feel about her. It was nearly impossible to miss. She exuded it! Her groundedness was palpable and exactly what I needed. I worked through every session feeling deeply rooted! Janine's qualifications were stellar. She was an expert, expert on trauma. It was her jam. I landed in the best hands. Thank you to the universe for, once again, leading me to my highest good! One of the most meaningful therapy sessions I had with Janine involved her throwing balled-up pieces of paper at me repeatedly! I was armed with a shield (a book we swiped off of her shelf). The exercise began with my writing down all the awful things that I say to/about myself in my head. Those voices were drowning out everything else, and it was keeping me stuck as if I were chained to a fence and could only move from there. I was in a circle with a very limited radius. Once I generated those automatic thoughts and ideas, we proceeded to ball/wad up copy paper. Before starting, Janine helped me 'craft' three responses to the words that inwardly assault me every day. They were pretty simple/short and sweet, and they needed to be as they would become my verbal rejection of the paper projectiles that were about to be thrown at me. The idea was to create a set of positive replacement thoughts that would become as automatic and show up as swiftly as the insults did. So, if "I am pathetic" was the old thought, Janine used it as verbal ammunition, she voiced while mounting her paper attack at me. My job was to swat it away with the book and yell, "I am growing." Any of my three new responses could be used against any one of the things being thrown at me. We started and Dr. Shelby wound up and threw the first paper ball, yelling, "You're pathetic!" and my job was to swat it away with my book as I yelled one of my replacement thoughts/phrases. She started slowly but increased her speed and did not stop. As her pile dwindled, she would collect the ones she already used and hurl them at me again. I am not sure how long we did this, but by the end, I was exhausted, and the replacement thoughts came as quickly as the insults did in my head. This is how I began learning to silence the automatic barrage of negative thoughts and ideas I was allowing to take up residence in my head. Dr. Shelby found ways of engaging every bit of me in therapy with astounding results! My body, my brain, my heart and my soul were all working together to heal together! In MY therapy space, I was working in ways I could never have imagined. Dr. Shelby, you made it possible to do the work toward healing!

I found Jessica Oifer through the *Psychology Today* therapist finder tool on their website. Jessica's introduction of herself and her practice spoke to me. Upon meeting her, I immediately knew I would be working with her toward healing. Jessica gave me permission to work on ME! Only me. Not my relationship, not the communication piece or the intimacy piece, which I had done in therapy before, but to dedicate the therapy time and space to myself! For years, I lived as the identified patient. It was me that needed fixing and to get well in order for everything to be ok. The narrative was that my past was driving my present, and if things were going to get better, I had to get better. While not totally untruthful, it was a lie. I still had work to do, there was no denying that, but the work was personal and not to make things better for or with others. The first time we met, she asked me why I was seeking out therapy. I answered by saying something to the effect of, "I am here to save my marriage." Her response was a gift that I carry with me today. I still use the wisdom she imparted that day. She offered the idea that I, in fact, was NOT there to save my marriage. I was there to work on myself and the things that were holding me back and see how that impacted my relationship. During my first session, I also told her that if she 'saw something clearly' to tell me. I did not want to be left circling the bowl, trying to figure it out myself. I had no time for that! While there is value to those 'ah-ha' moments when you put together all the pieces, and you can finally see how the last one fits into the puzzle, I also know the value of hearing from someone else what they see and suspect and trying it on to see if it resonates. I also told Jessica that I needed homework and to be held accountable. I knew if that were not part of our deal, I would leave her office, and return to life, forgetting all about the session until I was back at her door the following week. Thankfully, she agreed to all of my 'demands.' That alone made the therapy space mine and allowed me to be productive and proactive. It was because of Jessica that I developed a mindfulness practice, which allows me to amplify, survive to thrive in my day-to-day life. I learned to 'be.' To sit still and not run from the 'unpleasant.' I began to be curious about the thoughts and feelings that arose during those moments of stillness. I started to notice and curiously question. One of my favourite things to ask myself is (if I was in my head), "What do your heart and body think?" and then just listen and be curious about what comes up. I would do the reverse if I was connected to my body, but my mind was missing from the equation. Mindfulness brought calm, stillness, grounding, awareness, grace, kindness and, at times, even 'knowing' within me. I wish I had better words for it because it sounds so cliche, but if I am describing the value it brought to my life, these are the words I have to use.

It was not easy to live in the calm after a lifetime of chaos. It took dedication and many bargaining sessions within my head to embrace and evolve with it. My practice looks unlike any other, of that I am certain. My mindfulness practice is, well, mine. I set reminders on my phone throughout the day that remind me to check in and make sure I am being mindful! I rarely meditate right after waking up, and when I do meditate, I have a whole host of things that engage all of my senses (a candle, music and a smooth rose quartz crystal that I keep cold in my refrigerator until I need it) and I do not necessarily do the same things from day to day. For a very long time, I avoided mindfulness because it did not fit or feel right, and that was apart from the discomfort of being fully present (especially after compartmentalizing and dissociating for so many years). The rules about what it is 'supposed' to look like and how it 'should' be done held me back, as did a lack of understanding. First, mindfulness is not about clearing your mind, and for me, neither is meditation. My mindfulness practice (how I was taught) is about having thoughts, not emptying the thoughts from my head. Having thoughts and feelings and being aware of them in the moment, noticing and acknowledging them. It is being tuned into the subtle signals my body gives me throughout the day. Ultimately, it needs to be something that worked for me in order to stick with it.

To date, learning to be aware and present is some of the most important work I have done. In fact, at the start of the COVID-19 pandemic (around March 2020), I called Jessica, as I no longer held a weekly appointment, to say "Thank you" to her. At this point, I was divorced and living alone with my two cats (insert crazy cat lady comments here). The work we did allowed me to comfortably follow the restrictions that were mandated as measures to fight the pandemic (the growing number of cases and deaths around the world due to COVID-19). Being alone was comfortable. In the chaos of the outside world, I found calm and clarity in being alone. I actually enjoyed and experienced a tremendous amount of personal growth during the alone time the pandemic had created BECAUSE I had done this work with Jessica. I was able to easily 'be.'

NOTE: I write this and must acknowledge that I am not always happy or grateful. I have times when I struggle with remaining positive and even functioning. There are days (and periods of time when I am brought to tears by the deep sense of gratitude that I experience, and there are times when the tears are brought on by rage, how unfair the world feels, anger, and not wanting to always 'work so hard.' Finding mental wellness is not some magic, fix-it-all cure. It is not something that you arrive at and stop. For me, it is a commitment to return to the things I know to be true and helpful for me, even when I do not want to. It is giving myself credit when I finally shower after three days rather than being mad at myself for allowing it to get to that point in the first place. It means acknowledging that "this is how I feel NOW" and giving myself praise for the things I am doing (feeding the cats, drinking water, watching TV) rather than focusing on what I am not doing. It is throwing away the elaborate scoring/grading constructs that my old self would regularly use to find "evidence' to support the idea that I am failing and pathetic. It means that EVERY time I am knocked back down into my 'hole' that I look around and, in the darkness, find a taller ladder than I did the last time I ended up in this G-d awful pit of 'give-up' that has gotten deeper from the last time I visited. It is using that ladder to climb back out, even with the belief that I will end up down there again (this is a visualization exercise that I engage in — in great detail and with all the energy I can muster). It means knowing who I am and allowing myself to be human! When the darkness and despair are so familiar, it becomes hard to see that sadness, frustration, and doubt are part of the process (of course, for people like myself who live with depression, this is a far scarier place than for more chemically balanced people that I like to compare myself to), but I have done it, and I do 'practice what I preach.' I know and accept that feeling the 'awful' means that I also get to experience the 'fantastic.' I recognize and can distinguish the two because they ARE familiar. Again, when you live with depression, this is a much harder narrative to believe in and connect to. I have been and still live in that world. It is never a matter of choosing to be happy. If that were the case, prescription anti-depressants would be a thing of the past. In my experience, however, there is value in choosing to acknowledge the good, even when that good is really hard to find.

Dr. Janine Shelby

Retired from Clinical practice

Jessica Oifer-Stelle M.A., LMFT

http://www.jessicaoifermft.com/

(424) 384-3772

Dr. Suzanne Drake

Tools, Lessons learned and 'Words from Experience'

I am not a mental wellness professional. I have no licensing or higher degree in the field. What I do have, and can offer, is my personal experience, which should not take the place of reaching out to a qualified mental wellness provider. I am not sharing my experiences or the tools that have brought me to this time in my evolution as a means of medical advice or endorsement.

My personal Toolbox includes the 'what works for Nancy' items I have discovered over time. While there may be commonalities between my toolbox and someone else's, each person has to create their own unique set of 'what works for me,'

1. Mindfulness, setting intentions and a daily gratitude practice.

2. Journaling.

3. Community! Connections to people.

4. Sharing my story. Talking with others.

5. Finding gratitude for all of it.

6. It is an ugly, snotty knock-down, drag-out process. Do not fault yourself for the two steps forward and one step back. It was crying myself to sleep on the floor and listening to myself sob so intensely that I sounded like a wounded animal. It was feeling like the tears would never stop, but they did. I felt broken beyond repair, but I was not. I thought I was better off dead; nothing was further from the truth!!!!

7. Connect with nature.

8. Read books, listen to podcasts, watch shows, join groups that inspire (do not have to be about abuse), stories about resilience, hope after defeat, including the ugly parts. Gwendon Doyle's "*Untamed*" sparked something in me that I wished existed and made me realize it did exist and that it was in me all along.

9. Do things for others.

10. Check your self-talk. Your Brain Believes You- It is really that simple.

My word: Abundance

When we live with the belief that there is more than enough for all of us, we show up for one another in extraordinary ways! We build up rather than tear down. We celebrate rather than criticize. When we live in abundance we are constantly reminding ourselves of the hope, the possibilities and the certainty that what we desire has already happened; we are just catching up to it!

My Quote:

"*There is no agony like bearing an untold story inside of you,*"~Maya Angelou

I believe we all have a powerful and important story. When we allow them to live only inside of ourselves we are forced to wear masks and can only present a certain version of ourselves to the world. Sharing our stories gives others permission to do the same. Stories are affirmations we gift to one another.

Nancy Barrows M.S CCC SLP

Grew up in NY

GW---UCLA

Speech language pathologist 20 years (public school and private practice)

Named one of the Top 50 Most Impactful People of LinkedIn2021

Sharing her story and shaking things up!

Book your FREE 15-minute consultation HERE: calendly.com/nancybarrows

Known as the Queen of Engagement and named one of the Top 50 Most Impactful People of LinkedIn out of nearly 1 Billion business professionals, Nancy Barrows is a 20+ year Entrepreneur of a thriving private practice, Educator, Keynote Speaker and Coach who helps others understand the value and power of personal content on social media.

Using her 20+ years of experience and expertise in the area of Social Cognition, Nancy developed her program, *The Chick with the Toolbelt*, which helps individuals and companies meet their highest potential. She partners with clients on showing up, finding their voice and fully engaging their community across platforms and media, guiding them to reach their personal and business growth goals and build robust revenue streams - while sharing tools to maintain these changes independently.

Nancy has been highlighted on ROKU TV, LinkedInLIVE, Apple Podcasts, Spotify, YouTube, Twitter, Anchor, Google Podcasts, Stitcher, Amazon Music, Audible, VoiceYourVibe.com and more! She is LIVE every Wednesday and Saturday with Brian Schulman for their Global Award-Winning Live Shows: *What's Good Wednesday* and *Shout Out Saturday*, which have been featured on NASDAQ, Forbes, Thrive Global, Yahoo Finance, ROKU TV, Amazon Fire, The CW, multiple #1 best-selling books and syndicated on a SmartTV Network. Nancy is also the creator, host and executive producer of her own Live show, *Connected Human Conversations*.

Nancy has thrived through adversity and employs her experience to help others find their voice. By telling her story and creating the #RadiatingReal movement, she is making a positive impact and encouraging and inspiring others to do the same.

SOCIAL MEDIA HANDLES

Connect with Nancy Barrows on all social media channels via:

https://linktr.ee/voiceyourvibe

Linkedin: https://www.linkedin.com/in/nancybarrows/

Linkedin Company Page:

https://www.linkedin.com/company/thechickwiththetoolbelt/

Twitter: https://twitter.com/NancyDebra2

Instagram:
https://www.instagram.com/vibing_with_nancy_debra/

Facebook: https://www.facebook.com/nancy.l.barrows

YouTube: https://www.youtube.com/channel/UC87OpZBfiR-khSvDjI12JqA

TikTok: https://www.tiktok.com/@nancy_debra?lang=en

Look for #RadiatingReal on all social posts

IF I CAN, YOU CAN

By Aly Francis

I would grab a lighter, flick it, and hold the flame for about 10-15 seconds. Then I'd pick a spot on my arm and press it down. Alternatively, I would find a safety pin or razor blade and start making lines up and down my wrists and arms. These were my chosen methods of self-harm, and like many others, I still have the scars to this day. I became consumed in self-loathing, anxiety, depression and suicidal ideation at the age of 13. And many times since then, I thought to just end it all. I am still surprised sometimes that I made it to where I am now. So how did I get to that dark place?

At the age of 9, I became a child of divorce. Everything I had known, my church, my school, had all been uprooted. I experienced bullying all through my school days. My mother remarried a year after the divorce, and my sister and I couldn't stand the new 'step-thing.' My real father virtually became invisible. My mother has a narcissistic personality disorder and blamed everything on my sister and me and pitted us against each other. I became the scapegoat and 'black sheep' of the family while my sister became the golden child.

At the age of 12, I was already having symptoms of severe depression and anxiety. I began to cry all the time and suffered from night terrors and insomnia as well. I also suffered three ankle dislocations, six knee dislocations, and three knee surgeries between the ages of 12 and 21.

At 13, I had started self-harming. At 15, I stopped eating almost completely, and developed severe stomach pains. My mother started taking me to the first 'shrink' at 12 for the night terrors. Then at 15, she took me for more tests and therapy. After CAT Scans and a whole host of tests, I finally found a therapist who discovered I was having panic attacks in addition to depression, suicidal ideation, and anorexia. At 17, he prescribed me the anti-depressant drug Paxil. This was in 1995 before we had any of the warnings today about these types of drugs. While the drug did curb some of the anxiety, it actually increased my depression and suicidal ideation.

At the age of 15, I had also entered into adult relationships and had my first 'real boyfriend' and sexual experience, which of course, was toxic. Then I had my first first 'real love' right after that, which lasted about two years. However, during that time, he cheated on me repeatedly. Towards the end of my Senior year, he left me for a girl in our church youth group and at the ripe age of 18 and 19, they got married. I thought I was going to die when he left me. I had no idea at the time that I was suffering withdrawal from a narcissistic relationship. That same year at a party with kids from my school, my girlfriend and I were drugged and date raped. My memory of the whole event is like watching snapshots flash by in my mind.

By the time I was in my first semester of college, I had gained 75 pounds, thanks to the drug Paxil and my severe depression and trauma. My thoughts of suicide and acts of self-harm had only increased at this point. So I started skipping classes, and at almost 19, I dropped out and went to visit my father, who now lived just outside of El Paso, Texas. Big mistake. More partying, more getting in with the 'wrong crowd,' more trying new drugs, and more sexual trauma. I even had a shotgun pointed at my head one night. I honestly look back and can't believe I made it out of that town alive.

I had to swallow my pride and call my mother to move back up to NY. I can't tell you how much I did not want to do that. I also enrolled at a different college to try again. I soon started smoking cigarettes and pot again and snorted coke once in a while. I dropped out again. Do you see a pattern here? I was stuck in a trauma cycle, as so many of us are, that you cannot see when you are in it. I was constantly trying to heal my childhood wounds of not being good enough for my mother, of not being loved or supported, and of never feeling safe or secure. I was looking for love in all the wrong places, never realizing I had to love myself first.

That Summer, when I turned 20, I met my daughter's father. Well, technically, ran into him again. We had dated very briefly in high school for about two months. I would spend the next eight years in an on-and-off toxic relationship with him. He lied, cheated, partied, and put me through hell. Just after the summer of my 21st birthday, I took a pregnancy test and bingo! I naively thought he would want to change and we would be a happy family. However, nothing could have been further from the truth.

I loved my baby girl with every ounce of my being. I was so elated to be a mother. But I still had major trauma that was unhealed, along with major anxiety and depression. I had been on no medication and in no therapy for years now. Then bang! Post-partum depression hit me like a truck! Not only that but when she turned four months old, I was told of his infidelity during and after my pregnancy. I left him for a while. However, being alone terrified me more than anything else. Feeling unloved and alone killed me. My depression just got worse, and I let him back into my life again. I was still trying to work and finish school at the local community college. But trying to do all these things with severe anxiety and depression is just overwhelming. When he wanted to go to Rave parties on the weekends or try a new party drug, I was right there with him. We tried every drug, from Ketamine to Crystal Meth to Cocaine to Ecstasy to 'Molly' to 'Acid' and A TON of POT. It got to the point where we sold anything and everything of value we ever had to get more drugs. However, I never did drugs when I had my daughter with me. She was my only reason for living.

However, unbeknownst to me, my mother was already devising her plan to take my daughter from me. It's too long of a story to tell here, but just before my daughter turned two, my parents got full custody of her. Nothing has ever been as horrific as the day they came to take her. The one person in the world I thought I should be able to trust and rely on, my own mother, took my only child, my only love. My beautiful precious child. And I died inside. I wanted to kill my mother and then kill myself. Very shortly after, I gathered up all the drugs we had around and took them, not caring if I ever woke up again. By the grace of God or Angels or whatever you may believe in, I didn't take enough drugs to kill me. Instead, I agreed to the court's terms and enrolled in a 28-day rehab at a nearby hospital. I completed rehab and found my passion. I wanted to help others heal from trauma and addiction. I also completed parenting classes and therapy sessions so I could at least regain partial custody of my daughter. I left her father for good when she was almost seven. Just before she turned 10, and I was about to be 32, I was feeling pretty good. I had a steady job at an accounting firm, and I was going to school online to get an accounting degree. I had my own apartment. Life was getting decent and steady.

And then, I entered into my next long-term relationship with a man I worked with. Another mistake. Another narcissist. I stayed for 6 and 1/2 years, lying to everyone and to myself that this was love. We were even engaged for 4 of those years. It was all a lie. He cheated, lied and controlled my every move. I started drinking wine after work every day to deal with the stress. My daughter could see how unhappy I was. And I thought, "What kind of example am I being to her?"

So I left him. I moved in with my parents, where my daughter was still living part-time, and we lived there together for the next three years. Meanwhile, I still had unhealed trauma I was unaware of. I ended up in an affair with a married man at my next job. No, I'm not at all proud of this. He did not wear his wedding ring at work and told everyone he was separated, and he was trying to file for divorce. Well, about a year in, I found out that was all lies. Women at my work started telling me how they were not really separated, and he had had multiple affairs with multiple women at that job and had told them all the same type of lies. I believed his lies, and even when I confronted him or caught him red-handed, believe it or not, it still took me another year to break it off finally. He was the worst kind of narcissist I had encountered yet. A true wolf in sheep's clothing. He love-bombed me from day one, then devalued and discarded me like I was nothing. The relationship literally almost cost me my sanity. I was absolutely devastated, to the point where I found myself self-harming again in the bathroom at work and thinking of suicide. At the same time, I ran out of money to finish school and defaulted on my school loans. But they say, "It takes something to break you to truly awake you." That is still one of my favourite quotes to this day because it's true. I realized I was still not being the mother to my child that I wanted, nor loving myself or valuing myself at all. I knew it was either time to fight or just give up. However, little did I know that fighting to heal myself and break the trauma cycle I was in would involve four more years of craziness.

That year, the Summer of 2017, I cut that narcissistic jerk out of my life completely, quit that job, sold my car and anything I had of value, cashed in my 401(k) early, and booked a month long trip to Dublin, Ireland with my daughter, who graduated from highschool that summer as well. The plan was to get employment over there, enroll her in school and stay overseas for at least a couple of years. I want people to know that you can relocate overseas if you wish; it just takes some work. I had found a job, or so I thought before we left. However, literally a day before we got on the flight, it fell through. And after spending $4,000 for airfare and a room that I would not get back, we decided to take the trip anyways. After a beautiful month, we had to fly back to the USA, but we both did not want to return to NY. I still needed time to really heal.

So we went to live with my father in a tiny town in Pennsylvania. My daughter had never even gotten the chance to know her grampa, heck I hardly knew him either. However, shortly after we moved in, I relaized that this toxic cycle I was stuck in was not just because of my mother. My father was a covert narcissist as well and had major martyrdom and victim mentality. He also lived in such a tiny town I was unable to find work. So after a little over a year, we took another big chance and rented a car and moved to Cape Cod, MA, to stay with a girlfriend I met on Facebook. Yes, I know what you're thinking. How dumb can you be to take that chance without even meeting the person first? And you wouldn't be wrong. I will never do that again. I got a job immediately, which was a blessing, and she said she would let us live with her for six months with minimal charge, so we could save up to move out by May. Within two weeks she stated I had to give her half of my paycheque or get out. Within a month after that, she told us we had a week to get out because her mother was going to move in with her. We had no money saved at all in such a small amount of time. We ended up having to take a taxi to a homeless shelter an hour away. It was a nightmare. We were terrified. We posted a plea for help on Facebook, and my daughter's cousins came to get us.

So back to NY, we came full circle. When we got there, we knew this would be no picnic either. There were already six of them living in the home, plus their 18 animals. No exaggerating! It was literally a zoo. And a zoo they did not clean. I had never seen anything like it in my life. There were bird and dog feces and urine literally everywhere. We were stunned. And we were shoved into a corner of their basement on an air mattress. Our health was deteriorating, my knee problems were returning, and my daughter had anemia and kept having fainting spells. With no car as well and no public transportation, it was virtually impossible for either of us to work. So I cleaned their entire house to earn our keep as we figured out what we could do. In the meantime, we were now in the heart of the Covid Pandemic. We moved in with them in March of 2019, and this was now the Summer of 2019. As everyone was struggling at that point, they gave us until September to get jobs or get out. Everything was closed down! I still had no vehicle and no public transportation. Once again, we were facing homelessness.

So in September 2020, we left what little possessions we had left, took my beloved cat to a foster home, and checked into a shelter downtown. We spent 30 days in the 'emergency dormitory' with just 16 beds and a shared bathroom. They serve three meals a day if you could call them that. But we were then blessed to be accepted into what they call the 'Transitional Housing Program', which lasts up to two years. There was some bullying and some drug use, and some not-so-nice things to face, but I had heard other shelters were combined with men and women, which was way worse. We were lucky this was a women-only shelter.

Let me tell you, Divine Timing and Divine Orchestration are real my friends. Arriving at the shelter during the Covid-19 Pandemic was a huge blessing for us. We did not have to go through half the paperwork and interviews and trouble you normally have to go through to get public assistance. We got our food stamps, cash assistance, and Medicaid (government healthcare) immediately. We had all of our basic needs provided for, and we were even able to receive free education. We have been here for one year and two months now. I was able to become a Certified Peer Specialist, and I am now working for an agency that helps the homeless and those struggling with drug addiction. I can now use this certification to obtain a counselling degree which is exactly what I wanted but couldn't afford to do on my own. I also now have the first-hand experience to be able to relate to those I wish to help. I am able to help so many people now because I can uplift them through my story. In addition, we were able to get the medical attention we needed. My daughter is now healthy enough to attend school for computer technology, and I couldn't be more proud of her or more thankful for this shelter. We have also just received our Government Housing Vouchers and are finally moving into our own apartment.

This will be my favourite holiday season ever in my life! Just me, my daughter and my kitty together in our own home.

This crazy journey has forced us to face and integrate our shadow selves, to see and break the generational trauma cycles we were in, and to heal our wounded inner child. It's not easy. This past four years were probably the hardest thing I've ever faced, even though the 40 years before that were no picnic either!

Was this how I imagined my life would go? No. Did I think this is what would happen when we jumped on that plane to Ireland? Absolutely not. But would I go back and change anything now? Nope. It took me many years to be able to get to the place where I could stop wishing to turn back time. You can't possibly know, my friends, that if you could go back, anything would've turned out better. Or worse. Not only that, but I believe every single step is a part of your purpose. You did the best you could at the time with the knowledge you had. So stop beating yourself up! Every moment in life is an opportunity to grow. Besides that, you don't know what an impact your story could have on someone else's life one day. And now I see this most recent 'Tower' moment, where everything fell apart, and we ended up in a homeless shelter in the middle of a global pandemic, as the biggest 'miracle in disguise' in my entire life. Not only did it take care of our physical needs and safety, but it led us to a true healing of ourselves on all levels. In addition, it puts us on our path toward our true purpose.

Not only was I blessed with a beautiful friend that offered me this amazing opportunity to contribute to this book, but I was also able to develop and institute a class on cptsd and trauma recovery for the women here at the shelter that will now continue long after we have moved. In addition, I am working on a couple of my own books I hope to have published one day.

I no longer self-harm. I am 16 years in recovery from drugs. I take no antidepressants. I have no more suicidal thoughts. I can finally wake up each morning and look forward to what the day will bring me. I can finally say with all honesty that I like myself and am on my way toward truly loving myself!

So, in conclusion, I want to tell anyone reading this that if I can, you can too. At 44 years old. At 22. At 62. At any age or point in time! This, too, shall pass. You will get through this! There is a Divine Orchestration in everything. Your life has more meaning and purpose than you could ever possibly imagine. So I'll leave you with another favourite quote of mine, "Sometimes the smallest step in the right direction ends up being the biggest step of your life. So tip toe if you must. But take the step.' You can break yourself out of the trauma cycle, my friends. You can have the life you dream of! How do I know? Because if I can, You can! It only takes the first step. Believe in yourself. I believe in you.

Why I chose "Courageous" as my word of inspiration.

First, let me start by saying that to me, the word inspiration means helping people to see their potential when they can't see it in themselves. To motivate them to take action and look forward to creating a better future for themselves. That being said, I chose the word "Courageous" because until now, I have always thought of myself as anything BUT Courageous. So I want to inspire others by letting them know that if I can see how Courageous I am now, so can you. You have more strength and courage in you than you think you do. Just like the cowardly lion in the wizard of oz. None of them, the Lion, the Scarecrow, the Tinman or Dorothy, needed the wizard in the end, did they? Nope. Everything they needed was always within them the whole time.

All my perceived mistakes and bad choices in my life made me feel like a coward, a loser, and a quitter. Those terms my mother or peers often called me. But that is how we feel when we have no idea we are stuck in cycles of generational trauma. You were never born an 'addict' or a 'quitter' or a 'co-dependent' or any other derogatory or psychological term. You suffered from trauma in some form or another at some point in your life, no matter how big or small. Everyone has, in some form. You suffered hardships and trials, as we all do. And you did the best you could at that time with the knowledge you had. You were operating on a viral program of self-loathing and self-limiting beliefs. And I'm here to tell you that if you are still here, still fighting and trying every day, then my friend, you are Courageous!

If, like me, you have faced anxiety, depression, self-harm, addiction, suicidal thoughts, and you are still here, you are Courageous! If you have faced illness, poverty, grief and loss, bullying, catastrophes, and so on, you are Courageous. If you get up to go to a job you hate every day to put food on the table for your family. If you feel sick and in pain from chronic illness and still have to work and take care of others every day. If you continue to battle addiction and keep trying to overcome it no matter how many times it takes. If you are trying to leave that toxic situation or relationship. If you have decided to change careers and go back to school at any point in your life. If you keep getting up every day and have hope for what that day may bring, you, my friend, are COURAGEOUS!

It is possible to move on from merely surviving to thriving! And if you have chosen to fight for yourself, to try to heal, to try to love yourself, to break the chains of trauma cycles, to make every day count, then you are more Courageous than the cowardly lion. Now show the world how you Roar!

"Sometimes the smallest step in the right direction ends up being the biggest step of your life. So tip toe if you must, but take the step."-Naeem Callaway

"And He said to them, "Because of your little faith; for truly I say to you, if you have Faith the size of a mustard seed, you will say to this mountain, 'Move from here to there,' and it will move, and nothing will be impossible to you." -Mathew 17:20

Aly Francis

Aly is a 44-year-old single mother who was born in Indianapolis, IN but has lived most her life in Western New York. She has one beautiful 22-year-old daughter who is currently attending school for Computer Technology.

Aly holds a degree is Business Management and Accounting and has recently completed the Certified Peer Specialist certificate program. However, she now aspires to be a trauma recovery counsellor, life coach and published author. Her interests and passions have changed due to life experiences, and her goals now lie in helping humanity to overcome their traumatic experiences and live the healthiest lives possible.

She is all too familiar with narcissistically abusive relationships, having grown up in a toxic family environment and having a series of toxic relationships throughout her adult life. She has suffered from and been diagnosed with social anxiety, depression and c-PTSD. She has also struggled with self-harm, suicidal ideation and drug addiction. Currently, she and her daughter reside in a women's homeless shelter in their city. However, with faith, determination and hard work, she and her daughter have made tremendous personal and spiritual growth and are now on the path to health and wellness. They have received help with education and employment and will be moving into their own apartment this Christmas of 2021.

She hopes that by sharing her story of how she has overcome adversity and trauma, she can help others to do the same. Her ultimate goal is to show others that they are stronger than they think they are. She aims to teach them how to take back their power, discover their true authentic selves, and live their best, healthiest lives possible.

Amfrancis1347@gmail.com

Shining lights of hope in the shadows of religious extremism

By Junaid Qaiser

Hope in the shadow of Bias

Hope can be a powerful force in the face of bias and discrimination. When we are confronted with prejudice and injustice, it can be easy to lose hope and feel overwhelmed by the challenges ahead. However, it is in these moments that hope is most important.

By holding onto hope, we can stay motivated and continue to work towards a more just and inclusive society. We can draw strength from the stories of others who have faced bias and discrimination and who have fought for change and made a difference. And we can find hope in the small acts of kindness and compassion that exist in our daily lives.

It is important to remember that even in the shadow of bias, we are not powerless. We can take action to address bias and discrimination, whether through individual acts of kindness or by working with others to create systemic change. By coming together in solidarity and advocating for justice and equality, we can make a difference and create a brighter future for all. So let us hold onto hope and let it guide us as we work to build a more inclusive and just world.

Despite the challenges of growing up in an environment of religious bias and discrimination in my country, I always found hope in the words and creativity of my father, a renowned poet and intellectual. His passion for literature, modern contemporary thoughts and faith taught me the power of words to inspire change and uplift spirits, and his unwavering commitment to justice and equality served as a beacon of hope in times of adversity.

As I grew older, I became more aware of the social and political issues that plagued our community, and I began to use my own understanding of challenges and knowledge to make a difference. Drawing on my father's teachings and my own experiences of discrimination, I began writing and speaking out against religious intolerance and advocating for liberal values, human rights, democracy, and greater understanding of contemporary views and pluralism.

The issue of religious extremism in Pakistan has a long history, dating back to the Objective Resolution introduced in 1949, which sought to define the role of Islam in the country's governance. However, it was during the regime of General Zia-ul-Haq in the 1980s that religious extremism and intolerance became more widespread as he sought to Islamize Pakistani society and support the Afghan Mujahideen against Soviet forces.

Despite the end of Zia's regime, religious persecution and extremism continue to be major problems in Pakistan, taking many different forms. Minority religious groups, including Christians, Hindus, and Ahmadi Muslims, face discrimination and violence on a regular basis, and blasphemy laws are often used to target and silence those who speak out against religious extremism.

In addition, extremist groups like the Taliban and other militant organizations have carried out numerous terrorist attacks on civilians and security forces in the country, causing immense harm and destruction. These groups often use religion as a justification for their actions, but in reality, their actions go against the core principles of Islam and the values of the vast majority of Pakistanis.

Despite these challenges, there are also many Pakistanis who are working tirelessly to promote interfaith harmony, protect the rights of religious minorities, and counter extremist ideologies. These individuals and organizations offer hope for a more peaceful and tolerant future in Pakistan and demonstrate that the values of inclusiveness, compassion, empathy, and respect for all people can overcome the destructive force of religious extremism.

Pakistan has a number of laws that have been criticized for being discriminatory, including blasphemy laws that have been used to target religious minorities and stifle free speech. These laws, which carry severe penalties, including the death penalty, have been used to justify violence and persecution against individuals accused of blasphemy, often with little or no evidence.

In addition to blasphemy laws, Pakistan also has laws that discriminate against religious minorities in various ways, including denying them equal rights and opportunities in education, employment, and politics. These discriminatory practices have led to incidents of religious persecution, with religious minorities such as Christians, Hindus, and Ahmadi Muslims being targeted and attacked on a regular basis.

Despite the government's efforts to address these issues, religious persecution and discrimination continue to be major problems in Pakistan. There is a need for more robust legal protections for religious minorities, as well as increased public awareness and education about the importance of religious tolerance and respect for diversity.

Civil society organizations and individuals are playing a critical role in advocating for greater religious freedom and working to counter extremist ideologies that fuel violence and discrimination. By supporting their efforts and speaking out against discriminatory laws and practices, we can work towards a more just and inclusive society in Pakistan, where all people can live in peace and freedom.

I support such civil society organizations and individuals who are working to build a more liberal and inclusive Pakistan. These groups and individuals play a critical role in promoting human rights, democracy, and social justice, and their efforts are essential to creating a more equitable and peaceful society. By supporting these organizations and individuals through my writings and activism, I am helping to amplify their voices and raise awareness of the challenging issues they are addressing. I am hopeful through such contributing activism; we can build a brighter future for Pakistan and ensure that all of its citizens have the opportunity to thrive and contribute to their communities.

I have faced threats and discrimination, particularly during the Aasia Bibi case and Salman Taseer's murder. These were difficult and challenging times for many people in Pakistan, particularly those who were speaking out against extremism and advocating for greater tolerance and understanding.

It takes a lot of courage to stand up for what is right, especially when you are facing opposition and even danger. But by speaking out against discrimination and violence and by advocating for greater respect for diversity and inclusion, you are helping to create a better and more just society.

Through my efforts, I found that even small acts of bravery and compassion could have a powerful impact on the people around me. I discovered that hope is contagious and that by spreading positivity and empathy, we can create a brighter and more inclusive world. Though the challenges of discrimination and intolerance may still exist, I am filled with hope for a better future where we can all live together in peace and harmony.

It is worth mentioning here that Ms. Nadene Joy, the Founder and Chairperson of the Global Movement of Hope, has been playing a key role in keeping my hope alive for an inclusive new world. As a motivational speaker of hope, she has inspired many people to stay positive and optimistic, even in the face of difficult challenges.

One word of inspiration I'd like to share with you today is "Endurance," as I believe endurance is vital to remain hopeful as well as achieving our dreams. Endurance is a crucial trait when it comes to achieving our goals and keeping hope alive. It is the ability to persist and withstand challenges and difficulties over an extended period. Endurance helps us to stay focused on our goals, even when things get tough, and gives us the energy to keep moving forward.

When we face challenges, endurance helps us to keep pushing through and not give up. It is also essential in maintaining hope because it helps us to see beyond the present difficulties and look forward to a brighter future.

Endurance also allows us to develop resilience and mental toughness, which are necessary qualities for achieving success in any field.

Moreover, endurance is a critical trait for achieving success in life. It keeps hope alive by helping us to stay focused on our goals, even when things get tough. With endurance, we can overcome challenges and achieve our targets.

Nadene Joy's work with the Global Movement of Hope is focused on promoting positive change and building a better future for all. Through her speeches and advocacy, she encourages people to take action and make a difference, no matter how small or large their contribution may be. She reminds us that we all have a role to play in creating a more inclusive, just, and peaceful world.

In times of darkness and uncertainty, it can be easy to lose hope. However, by listening to voices like Nadene Joy's, we can find the strength and inspiration to keep moving forward and to work towards a better tomorrow. Let us continue to listen to the messages of hope and positivity that inspire us to create a more inclusive and just world.

Remember that hope is a powerful force that can help us navigate through difficult times and inspire us to work toward a brighter future. Hold onto hope, take action forward each day and know that you are not alone in your journey.

Junaid Qaiser

Junaid Qaiser is a social media influencer who is committed to human rights and contemporary values; he is using various platforms to amplify the voices of marginalized communities and work towards creating a more just and equitable society.

He is a South Asian-born writer, journalist and activist with experience in various industries, including online media, social media management, journalism, corporate communications, media production and newspaper publications. He is using his influence to advocate for policies and practices that protect human rights, democratic values and peace. This includes supporting organizations that work towards these causes, also using their platform to call for change, and engaging in dialogue with their followers to encourage action and engagement.

Junaid has developed a deep understanding of the political developments, project management processes, as well as the ability to analyze and interpret complex large-scale political and social questions. He is a strong community and social services professional, and he has been contributing to the movements for peace, rights and justice as a social media influencer who, for years, has been writing and speaking on human rights, liberal democratic values, religious harmony, and a peaceful and just world. His trenchant insights on liberalism, democratization, political, social and diplomatic developments have won him a large and loyal social media support. His writing features commentaries and analysis on political issues with a focus on human rights and liberal democracy; his liberal thoughts have brought awareness about important human rights issues and the importance of modernity in his country.

Junaid is also the Vice-Chair of The Global Movement of Hope and a Top Person Ambassador, an International Business, Politics and NGO magazine, and a Chief-Editor of a magazine.

LinkedIn: www.linkedin.com/in/junaidqaiser

Twitter: @JunaidQaiser

Facebook: Junaid.qaiser

Instagram: @junaidqaiser

RECOVERY IS A MARATHON

By Jody Salway

In 2006, as part of Task Force Orion (Operation Archer) to Kandahar, Afghanistan. From Feb. 2006 to Aug. 2006, we were continuously engaged with the Taliban. By the middle of 2006, the roadside bomb (IED), our contacts with the Taliban, and causalities on both sides sharply escalated. This brought our death toll up to 18 in just a few months.

It was only a few hours into the operation when a lull in the fighting had us feeling like this could go either way. We took this advantage and went on the offensive again; however, this time utilized American air assets to disrupt the Taliban's movement and defensive posture.

Early in the morning of July 17, an A-10 Warthog from a few hundred feet in the air dropped a 1000 lb JDAM (Joint Direct Attack Munition) on what it thought was Taliban insurgence. For some unknown reason, it landed in the middle of my Platoon. I've never experienced so much noise, dirt and debris as I did I that moment; so much force came up out of the ground after impact that I was shoved violently on my face, injuring my head, neck, back, and left clavicle (I had a death grip on my weapon so that's why the left side took most of the brunt).

I spent the next two days throwing up between small painful naps as we leaguered up in various locations and headed back to the Kandahar Airfield for debriefing and resupply. That was my first visit of many over the next decade and a half. I struggle to stay in the military due to the injuries, the nightmares, and the constant hypervigilance and distrust of my leadership.

By 2012, I moved to a small hobby farm in Montmartre, SK. And contrary to what we believed was a fresh new start, it wasn't, and it didn't fix anything; it made it worse. The nightmares and my behaviour started to get a lot of attention from my wife, who wasn't equipped to understand what was happening or how to get me help.

I started drinking heavily to cope with the nightmares and thought it would help me sleep. By the summer of 2015, I hit "Catastrophic Failure," and I was broken; my wife was barely hanging on, and we both knew it couldn't continue. I was doing things that would make it easier for my wife and family to leave me. I did this to avoid connecting with people that way; I never had to worry about letting them down or being killed. I lived a painful mantra: I will fail them, lose control, and don't deserve love.

I asked for help. Healing and recovery are tricky when you aren't sure what's wrong or where to start. I went through three doctors before I felt confident we could work together. Over the next eight years, my recovery was rocky, and I never seemed to get into a routine long enough to make a noticeable difference. So, I gave up. It wasn't till I was admitted to the hospital for a mental health breakdown that I understood what I needed to do.

I thought being in the hospital would get me the help I needed, except the first words from the Psychiatric Nurse's mouth were, "What do you expect us to do for you?" I realized: Nobody will care enough to do it for you. I am the common denominator in all of this. My recovery was mine alone, and it was time to take control. And I did, and to this day, I am glad I did. I learned a lot in this recovery journey: how to forgive myself for my mistakes and things outside my control.

To understand that everyone is going through something, so be more understanding. And that Post Traumatic Growth will happen! Negative experiences can spur positive change, including personal strength, the search for new possibilities, improved relationships, a new appreciation for life, and spiritual growth. We aren't sick, struggling, ill or injured; these are our new post-traumatic growth pains. And like any growth, it is very challenging to see the gains. It's there, and you'll know it when it happens.

There is a word that needs to be said: Uncomfortable. Nothing worthwhile is ever comfortable; recovery will sometimes be uncomfortable and humiliating, and humbling. But never comfortable. Being comfortable is a form of complacency, and complacency has no functionality in your recovery.

The determination needs to be all day, every day, a marathon of consistency.

Jody Salway

Jody is a former Canadian Forces soldier who has dedicated almost a decade of service in Canada and abroad. Jody deployed to Kandahar, Afghanistan, in 2006 as a section 2ic (second in command) with Task Force Orion, Op Archer. During this time, he was wounded in action during an intense offensive urban operation.

He suffered a Traumatic Brain Injury and was later diagnosed with PTSD. When he's not working, he dedicates his spare time to advocating for veterans and first responders who have PTSD. He now enjoys life in Regina with his wife Carole, Clover (his service dog) and 3 kids ... 4 kids if his wife is counting.

Jody Salway LinkedIn:

https://www.linkedin.com/in/jodysalway/

www.linkedin.com

MY HOPE

By Faye Marks

Hope you have when things go wrong,

And at times will make you strong.

It is a faith that better will come,

A faith we all share not just some.

Have a problem? Hope is there,

Even if no one cares.

Hope is something that keeps you going,

Through all the pain that you are knowing.

Hope will help you get through,

So many things you need to do.

It gives you strength throughout the day,

And makes you feel better in some way.

When you have hope there is a future,

You will get there I am sure.

Hope is what you have to live,

Hope is what makes you give.

Hope will take you through your life,

Hope will help you make it right.

If you had no hope, you see,

What a poor soul you would be.

- fem

I lost my husband almost two years ago, and it still seems as though it was yesterday. It is a very hard thing to lose someone you love so dearly. I cry almost every day as I miss him so much, but I know it was in God's plan. Though he will always be with me, there is a hope that a better person I will be. Things have happened that never would have been if he was still here on earth. I have met so many caring people and so many who have also lost a loved one. As I write poems to get my feelings out, I started writing poems about losing him. I now have a published book and friends I would never have had. I have also been able to help some of them through their grief as we share some of the same feelings. I keep busy making "memory" bears and have started making "memory dogs" also. God has blessed me in so many ways, and I am thankful for the years I had with my husband. I know he is gone, but I will always have him in my heart. I do know that there is hope and faith that things will be better. I know there is a future for me as I move forward, and there will be a future for you too. "For I know the plans I have for you," declares the Lord, "Plans to prosper you and not to harm you, Plans to give you hope and a future" Jeremiah 29:11

Faye Marks

Faye Marks was born in New London, WI, USA, the fifth of five children (all girls). She attended parochial grade school and graduated from New London High School. She met her husband in 1970 and married in 1972. He passed away in May of 2021. She is the mother of four children, nine grandchildren and two step-grandchildren. Her married life consisted of living and working on their farm in partnership with her husband's brother and family. It was a life of much joy, lots of laughter, unending work, and some really hard times. She worked various jobs throughout her life but was able to be a "stay-at-home" mom while her children were growing up. Throughout her writings, you will see her great love for God. Without Him, she would not have been able to weather through.

THE FOUR PILLARS OF UNITY

By Nadene Joy

In order to achieve complete unity, there are four concrete pillars in which we begin to orient ourselves and move towards in each passing moment. These four lasting, eternal pillars of Unity, as evidenced in the naming of this binary star, include:

1) Hope

2) Happiness and Joy

3)Peace and

4)Love

It is imperative to further identify each pillar in detail and outline its importance in the collective consciousness of all humanity in moving towards a more #united connected universe where we operate together in collaboration in unity and in community vs apart on our own and in competition with others.

Through the sharing of our stories like those shared throughout the compilation of this book, we move towards greater unity and connectedness with all of humanity as we recognize we are not alone in our journey and are a part of something and a purpose that is much greater than ourselves.

Hope is the first pillar and is the sole focus of this book. When we have Hope in our lives, we bring hope to others. Hope is the seed, the foundation and tree of life, which bears much fruit to those who have faith and believe in something greater than themselves. When we take action toward achieving our dreams and goals, we make hope, not just a dream but rather a perceivable reality. Hope is a seed that God plants in our hearts to remind us there are better things ahead that begin with the thoughts we choose and the choices we choose to make and act upon today. When you plant seeds of hope in your garden, or business, or life, there are no promises. However, there is an unfailing driving force that makes you persevere because you have hope and something to believe in that you will succeed, potentially far beyond your wildest dreams. Hope is the light that shines bright in the dark to illuminate our steps forward and the faith we surrender to and trust in something much greater than ourselves.

Hope with faith and taking action forward will transform the dark into the light. It is the smallest incremental steps taken consistently over time that make the greatest change. To summarize, Hope is Helping Other People Eternally Elevate. It all starts from the inside when we believe and have faith in something greater.

Happiness and Joy are the second pillars of unity, as when we have hope, it leads us to greater fulfillment, purpose and happiness and true joy. When we are focused on true, long-lasting everlasting joy and happiness from the inside out, this is what we are referring to within this pillar.

True happiness and joy are contagious and are spread like wildfire. Have you ever witnessed a laughing baby and how contagious it is to smile and laugh along with them? A smile may be a small gesture, but it has the power to change the world for the better, one smile at a time.

There are many components of joy which include the following additional seven pillars of joy: four pillars are qualities of the mind – **perspective, humility, humour, and acceptance,** and four are qualities of the heart – **forgiveness, gratitude/compassion, and generosity**. When we set our mind and heart on the above, we are more connected with the world and, therefore, more unified and joyful as a whole.

The third pillar of unity is Peace, referring to both internal and external peace. When we think of a peaceful environment or world, we often think of the word and feeling of being in a calm state of being with mutual respect and love for one another of all parties involved.

We constantly consciously and subconsciously strive for a greater, more peaceful world, society and existence. A culture of peace exists of **1) dismantling the culture of war, 2) environmental peace, 3) education for justice and compassion, 4) human rights education, 5) cultivating intercultural solidarity, and 6) harnessing inner peace.**

World Peace, in general, grows through topics of discussion and actions related to cohesive nonviolence, unconditional acceptance for self and others, fairness and greater effective, authentic communication.

Overall, Peace is the main characteristic and one of the foundations and roots of a civilized society. Peace must begin with each one of us starting today from the "inside out." Choose to let go of all that no longer serves you for your highest good and experience all of God's grace and peace from within the deepest depths of your heart and soul.

The fourth and last pillar of moving towards greater unity in our world and universe as a whole is Love. There is nothing greater in this world than pure unconditional love. Love is infinite with no limits or bounds; it conquers our greatest fears and heals our deepest disappointments and wounds from our past— love truly is the greatest gift of all.

A few pillars of love include mutual care and respect, mutual dependability, mutual trust and mutual sacrifice - it is the perfect balance of harmony and give and take, the yin and yang of our existence. Agape, unconditional love of God is the greatest level of love experienced, which also includes a greater awareness of humility, courage, faith, obedience, forgiveness, self-discipline, and gratitude with blessings and thanksgiving for all things, great and small.

Ultimately as J.K Rowling states,

"We are only as strong as we are united and as weak as we are divided." Together we are much stronger than we are apart. My prayer is for unity for all families, communities and nations worldwide, starting with you from the inside out.

"When there is no enemy within, the enemies outside cannot hurt you. – Winston S. Churchill

Overcoming Covid Through Hope and Faith: A Story of The Gift of Life in Uncertain Times

By JYE

Hope lives deep in your soul where you believe and have faith in the promises of God. John 3:16 *"For God so loved the world that he gave His only begotten Son, that whosoever believeth in Him should not perish, but have everlasting life."*

On September 9th, 2021, I went to work feeling great. An hour before the end of my shift, I started to feel extremely weak and nauseous and had to leave. By the time I got home, I was so weak and exhausted I dropped everything at the door and barely made it to my bed, where I stayed for several days.

I had no strength to get out of bed or to even move any part of my body and had to lie completely still flat on my back (Psalm 46:10 *"Be still and know that I am God."*) The slightest movement from any part of my body triggered a severe cough and shortness of breath, but I had HOPE that God would carry me through and give me the strength to make it. (Isaiah 43:2 *"God will carry you through the storm."*)

When I finally did try and get out of bed, I repeated over and over again, "The Lord is my strength," "The Lord is my strength" while making my way to the kitchen, and with God's help, I was able to get a glass of water and make it back to bed. After ten days, I was tested and received a text telling me I tested positive for COVID-19.

I was sick for several months, and thank God I am here today and am so grateful for the loving care and prayers from my daughter, grandchildren and many others. All their love and support meant the world to me and got me through some very difficult times. I

HOPE the following verses will give you the hope and strength they did me.

Philippians 4:13 *"I can do all things through Him who strengthens me."* Psalms 28:7 *"The LORD is my strength and my shield; my heart trusts in Him, and He helps me. My heart leaps for joy, and with my song I praise Him."* Romans 12:12 *"Rejoice in hope, be patient in tribulation, be constant in prayer."* Romans 15:13 *"May the God of HOPE fill you with joy and peace as you trust in Him."*

My daughter sent me a video of the song *Overcomer* by Mandisa, which I played over and over again. I know it will give you hope also.

"Watching people drive by T mac on the radio

Got so much on your mind Nothing's really going right Looking for a ray of hope

Whatever it is you may be going through I know he's not gonna let it get the best of you

You're an overcomer Stay in the fight 'til the final round You're not going under 'Cause God is holding you right now

You might be down for a moment Feeling like it's hopeless That's when he reminds you That you're an overcomer

You're an overcomer Everybody's been down Hit the bottom, hit the ground

Ooh, You're not alone Just take a breath, don't forget

Hang on to his promises He wants you to know The same man, the great I am

The one who overcame death Is living inside of you So just hold tight, fix your' eyes On the one who holds your life There's nothing he can't do He's telling you

You're an overcomer You're an overcomer So don't quit, don't give in You're an overcomer

Don't quit, don't give in You're an overcomer."

"May the God of hope fill you with all joy and peace as you trust in him, so that you may overflow with hope by the power of the Holy Spirit." My one word of inspiration for you is "**overcomer**" as no matter what you are going through, no matter how down you are and how hopeless you feel, don't give in to the lies of the enemy and never, ever forget you are an overcomer! BELIEVE, FAITH, TRUST and HOPE.

Faith is the hope of things unseen. Know that in your darkest moments, God will not abandon you. Trust in God through the trials you are facing.

Having faith in God is your hope and assurance that everything will be okay. God is your best friend. He is like the wind. We can't see Him, but we know he's there. Whatever you're going through doesn't define you. Your strength and courage do.

Never give up hope. Talk to God. 1 Peter 5:7 *"Cast all your anxieties on Him because He cares for you."* Give all your worries and cares to God. Believe in the goodness of the Lord. He will meet your every need. God wants you to come to him with your cares and concerns. When you put all your cares in His hands, he puts peace in your heart.

If you feel lost and alone, God knows exactly where you are and what you need. Salvation is by grace, through faith. There's nothing you've done, or ever can do, to deserve it. Salvation is a free gift from God. All you have to do is receive it! My prayer for you today is that God would touch you with his healing hand and meet your every need and give you the comfort and strength you need to get through whatever it is you're going through. In Jesus' name, I pray. With Love and Joy, All Glory to God.

JYE

CONCLUSION

Hope is all around us. When we take the time each day to pause long enough to increase our awareness of the world we notice the thoughts, words and actions that bring us Hope in so many experiences of life. If we are not careful to remain aware of our surroundings, it is also easy for us to lose hope and spiral downwards into despair. The good news is that we have a choice and can ultimately choose to elevate and bring greater hope to ourselves first and then others as we cannot pour from an empty cup. Change occurs through the actions we choose to take which also turns your hopeful dreams into reality. This is done by speaking life and greatness into the life's of others as Hope is the foundation and tree of life by God's miraculous grace alone. Your thoughts, words and actions truly matter and you have the power to bring hope to all you encounter. Challenge yourself to speak hopeful encouraging words and inspire at least one person everyday and together if we all did this even for the remainder of this year, this of what a radically different world we would live in for the better!

Stories unite and heal. When we authentically share our story, real-life experiences and lessons learned from our hearts of the many trials and tribulations we have faced in life, we positively change and transform lives to uplift the collective planet to greater love and connectedness and belonging. Simply by knowing and feeling like you are not alone and someone cares about you is one of the greatest treasures we posses. Take action and have the bold courage to share your story this week with someone. The first time you share your story will be scary as I speak from experience but I promise it will become easier with practice. Trust your gut instinct, your higher intuition and God's truth to show you the way and illuminate the path forward including each word spoken and good deed performed. You have everything you need inside out to speak truth from the heart in all circumstances and to boldly step forward everyday to live out your unique purpose in life and lead the way to inspire many to also do the same. It all starts with the first step. No matter what just keep going and moving forward everyday. It doesn't matter how big the step is, just keep the momentum moving forwards as even small steps compounded lead to monumental change over time!

Unity is the feeling of oneness- being united, being together in community, being undivided. Being a part of a community group, whether locally, or online globally is one way we can move towards greater unity for all and in turn bringing the four pillars of unity which begins with having greater 1) hope which in turn leads to an overall increased level level of 2)happiness and joy in each moment which fosters greater 3) peace and unconditional 4) love for self and all others which then brings more Hope and the Cycle of Unity continues on infinitely as a positive ripple of greatness. Challenge yourself to join a new community group this month that speaks to your heart and that is in alignment with your personal morals and values. You never know the lives you will touch and possibly even save by showing up and sharing your gifts, talents, lessons and stories with the works! Positivity, hope and love and kindness is contagious- let's commit to spreading it like wildlife across all nations as the world needs YOU. You matter and are a part of something so much greater.

Expect and be Open to the unexpected blessings in life. You just never know where the path will lead next on your journey called life. Who knows it might very well end up being something you never thought was humanly possible. Be open to the infinite possibilities that await and have hope not just tomorrow, but for today and know that with God anything is possible! Know when you help others and bring greater HOPE into the world you are not only helping yourself, you are also Helping Other People Eternally Elevate- a won-win for all!

Do not be afraid to dream and let fear paralyze you from living your greatest potential in life. Live in each moment as of it were your last with no regrets and as the Legendary Les brown says "too many of us are not living our dreams because we are living our fears." You have GREATNESS inside of you, never let anyone else's opinion of you dictate your reality!

Be the fire of Hope through taking action towards greatness everyday. Hope is the lifeline when we face struggles and uncertainty in life. You got this and will get through your current circumstances, keep believing, trusting and surrendering all to God the ultimate Creator of heaven and earth. When you believe, you will succeed —as with God ALL things are possible. Take courageous action each day towards the life of your dreams as if it's already happened as life is short and every moment truly matters.

"Hope without Action is like Fire without Fuel"

-Nadene Joy, Founder of The Global Movement of Hope

Nadene Joy

As a Global Royal Advisor, Leadership Strategist, Communications Expert, Business Accelerator, Executive Coach, Chair and Founder of The Lead 2 Impact Summit, Nadene Joy is also a Member of The International Society of Female Professionals, multiple international bestselling author and a CEC Global Ambassador. She is recognized internationally as a top sought after woman in leadership, known as the "Changemaker," who has been featured on hundreds of global media outlets including USA TODAY, FOX, CBC and The Globe and Mail and has worked with thousands of clients internationally and advised personally with some of the most prolific leaders of our time. Nadene Joy is also the recipient of The TISGS Award of Business Excellence In Social Impact in Dubai, Woman of Substance Award from The St. Mother

Theresa University in Australia, one of the recipients of The Top 40 Global CEO of The Year Award by Excellence Speaks, Ambassador for Human Rights and Peace, a certified NLP Practitioner, designated Professional Geologist (P. Geo.) and is one of a very select few women globally who was distinctively honoured to receive the Woman of Heart and Visionary of Hope Award (WOHA).

Nadene Joy is a remarkable world-class leader who is also a woman of positive impact and of faith who is passionate about serving all others, empowering our youth, is an impactful authentic leader, humanitarian and friend who makes a positive distinguished difference. She is fervently dedicated to increasing international mental health awareness along with bringing greater hope, joy, peace, purpose, clarity, unity and love in our world to all she encounters. Nadene Joy is a living example of hope, God's unconditional love, infinite possibilities and believes that "together we are much stronger than we are apart." It is through the successive collaborations and unity of many diverse communities globally that we will begin to move towards greater unity and unprecedented positive impact for so many others.

"Changing Lives through Changing Leadership"

Website: www.NadeneJoy.com

Email: Nadene@NadeneJoy.com

LinkedIn: http://linkedin.com/in/nadenejoy

www.NadeneJoy.com

www.theglobalmovementofhope.co

Hope Quotes

"*Hope without Action is like Fire without Fuel.*" -Nadene Joy

"*Hope alone will not do anything. Hope with will, a pure heart and goal setting will be the best way to succeed in everything.*" -Nadene Joy

"*Learn as if you will live forever, live like you will die tomorrow.*" — Mahatma Gandhi

"*The very least you can do in your life is to figure out what you hope for. And the most you can do is live inside that hope.*" -Barbara Kingsolver

"*By faith, everyone of us should graciously hope to receive something good. Having good people around is a treasure you hope for. A wonderful family, friends, partner, team, children, job and peace of mind are precious things we hope for to make our lives worth living. Many people use words like "I hope so!" This simply means that they are optimistic that their wishes will come through.*" -Anthony Ezeaputa, CEO of Canada Africa Network

"*Hope is being able to see that there is light despite all of the darkness.*" - Desmond Tutu

"*When you're told: You're not capable and To go away, When you believe: You have nothing to offer and You aren't worth it, When love: Crushes your heart and Looks the other way, When you know what pure love feels like: You do it anyway, and You move forward. That's hope.*" -Anna Taylor

"*Life is never made unbearable by circumstances, but only by lack of meaning and purpose.*" -Viktor Frankl

"*Hope - He is the Only Permanent Source to Eternity.*" -Elaine Ong

"*We all have different stories to tell, but the one thing that connects us is our ability to look forward to the things that we desire. Believe in yourself and in what you can do — stand your ground and never lose hope.*" -Unknown

"When I think of the word hope, I think of the acronym: Hold On Pain Ends. Hope means that no matter how tough the difficulties or challenges I am facing in the moment, the difficulties or challenges will eventually end or, at the very least, diminish in severity, that every moment turns into a new day that turns into a beautiful story of a life well lived. Hope gives you the courage and confidence to continue searching to find the light at the end of the tunnel, to find your purpose and to continue to fight a courageous battle of a continuous uphill climb with endless mental health struggles, to simply continue living life even for seconds at a time, when minutes, hours, and days seem like too much. Always remember, after every storm, a rainbow will appear, and for me that is hope." Love, Light, Peace -Ashley Boehme

"When people are able to go from they are to where they want to be, it makes the world more hopeful. It brings back faith in the future of humanity. This is where my heart lies and where my passion resides. Hope for Humanity. Helping Other People Excel." - Ron Johnson

"Hope means to continue looking forward to what God has for us — eternity and what He has in store for us next in this life here on earth." -Shawn Maves

"When we receive a glimpse of the glory of eternity, our pain is relativized in such a way that the present tribulation becomes "a source of hope" because we know it is happening in order to show God's glory at the end through our experiences." -Akko (Osaka, Japan)

"So we fix our eyes not on what is seen, but on what is unseen, since what is seen is temporary, but what is unseen is eternal." -2Corinthians 4:18

"Shoot for the moon. Even if you miss, you'll land among the stars." - Norman Vincent Peale

"Hope to me is the bridge between worlds. The energy of soul sovereign faith. That takes us into new pastures of existing and collectively bringing us home as humans." -Kathleen Dutton

"Hope is replaced by possibility to take out the inaction and make it actionable as without taking action we cannot manifest anything." -Nader Sab